A *Mother's* Journey

MINNIE BELLE WEBB

ISBN 979-8-88685-017-8 (paperback)
ISBN 979-8-88685-018-5 (digital)

Christian Faith Publishing
832 Park Avenue
Meadville, PA 16335
www.christianfaithpublishing.com

Printed in the United States of America

To all my children whom I love very much
Gwen, Bertha Dee, Adele, Fred Allen, Wayne,
Jimmy, Judy, Robert, Eddie, and Debbie

Minnie Belle and Fred

A Mother's Journey

Now that I am in my eighties and the Lord has reminded me many times to write down my memories, I thought I would try. I know I can't remember everything, nor do I want to. Some things are buried too deep to remember, but many things are still clear in my mind. God has always been so very good to me, and I love Him.

I was born on March 3, 1916, in Cullman County, Alabama. I was the ninth child of Wilburn R. Palmer and Nora Jane (Townsend) Palmer. I have four brothers—James, Jesse, William, and Brady. I have five sisters—Nettie, Rosa, Mae, Echoe, and Jewell. My mother was a very pretty lady with black hair and blue eyes. I loved to hear her sing; she had a lovely voice. My dad was also a handsome man with black hair and blue eyes.

I never met my grandfather Palmer (he died as a young man) or my grandmother Palmer. She lived to be over one hundred years old. They lived in Georgia.

I loved my grandfather Townsend, but he was a hard man to love. Sometimes he was a lot of fun to be around. My grandmother Townsend was a very sweet lady. My mother looked a lot like her. She lived with my mother's brother, Uncle Charlie, several years before she died. She was a religious lady.

My grandfather Townsend remarried. He married a nice Christian lady much younger than him. They had one daughter, Mary. She is a few years younger than me. I love her very much.

My parents met in a cotton field. My mother was picking cotton one day when she was fifteen years old. My daddy was picking up the baskets of cotton and emptying them in the wagon. When he came to my mother's basket, he asked her if she would marry him when she was sixteen, and she told him she would. When she was sixteen, they slipped away and got married. When Granddaddy found out about it, he went and got her, and it was several weeks before they got back together. I loved my mom and dad very much.

They owned a large farm and a nice home in Alabama. They grew cotton, corn, and grain for their livestock. They lived there several years until all of us children were born, except my youngest brother.

When I was just walking good, all the family except my little sister, Jewell, and Mom were in the field picking cotton. My mom was washing clothes that day, and she had a large family to wash for. They didn't have washers and dryers in those days. She had a rubboard, tubs, and a big black kettle to boil their water and some of their clothes in. Then they would hang them on a line in the yard to dry. Probably, they would sprinkle their clothes down until damp and iron them the next day with a flat iron heated on top of the kitchen range. My mom was a very busy lady.

That day my brother Jesse came to the barn to get the cotton frames for the wagon so they could put more cotton in it. I saw him, but my mom didn't. I followed him into the barn hallway. He had already gone up into the loft, and he did not know I was there. When he threw the frames down, one of them hit me on my head, knocking me unconscious and fracturing my skull and cutting a large gash on the left side of my head. When he came down from the loft, that is how he found me—bleeding and unconscious. We were around fifteen miles in the country, no telephone, and nearly all the family members were in the field. Doctors drove buggies with horses in those days and were scarce.

My mom said she cleaned the incision the best she could and filled it with yellow sulfur and then she prayed. God heard her prayer and saved me. That is my first miracle. Praise His holy name.

I still have the scar and dent in my skull to remind me. I have always wondered why people built their barns so close to their house in those days. Maybe it's because they would not have so far to walk in the wintertime to care for their stock.

My granddaddy Townsend sold his farm and moved to Tennessee. He kept writing to my parents to sell their farm and move also. He said it was a beautiful place, and he wrote like money grew on trees. Finally, my parents sold everything and moved, but they never found the trees the money grew on, just hard work and share-cropping. They never owned another home, and we moved around a lot after that.

We first moved to Ethridge, Tennessee. That is where my grand-daddy lived. I was around four years old then. I kind of remember that first house we lived in. It was a two-story house with a climbing rosebush on the front porch. I do remember a scorpion jumping from the rosebush onto Rosa's shoulder and almost scaring her to death. I remember a persimmon tree close to the house, and they were ripe. One day, Bill, Jewell, and I went to the tree. Bill got up into the tree and shook them off, and they filled my skirt with ripe persimmons and dripping juice. I went to the house like that.

My mom had company, and they were sitting on the porch. When she saw me, she was so embarrassed. She gave me a good spanking, and I never did that again. She still let us get the persim-mons and take them to our little neighbor. She was an elderly lady who lived by herself in a little log house. She dried them for winter use, and she said they were real good. I don't know; I never ate any.

The next year, we moved farther out into the country. Jewell started going to school while we lived there. My older sisters would take me to visit sometimes. One day, Jewell's teacher told her class the one who could spell *Baby Ruth* the next day would be given a piece of chocolate candy. My sisters taught me how to spell *Baby Ruth*, and I went to school with Jewell that day. I was the only one who remembered how to spell *Baby Ruth*, and she gave me two pieces of candy. I gave Jewell one of them. That was a real treat back then.

My youngest brother, Brady, was born while we lived there. I cried and cried because he took my place, and I could not sit on my mom's lap and be the baby. I soon got over it, and he was always so precious to me.

When he was about seventeen months old and walking good, my mother's brother and his wife came to visit us. They stayed a couple of weeks, and while they were there, she and mom cut and made her a new dress. There was a piece left and some big scraps. She forgot to take them when she went home. I told mom she had given them to me. I lied. I begged my mom until she cut and made Brady a little apron out of them. He looked so sweet in it. At that time, little boys wore little aprons with a belt in the back. My conscience hurt me so bad every time she put it on him that I would almost get sick. Then one day, I was outside playing, and I saw Uncle Cleve coming down the path toward our house. I just knew why he was there. I ran in the house and told mom I had lied to her about that material, and I ran outside and hid until he left—almost all day. I was hungry and tired. I never got a spanking for that; my conscience had whipped me enough. I have never lied that way again. She had washed her dress, and it shrank, and she needed the material to put a piece around the bottom to make it longer. I still hate I did that.

While we lived close to Granddaddy Townsend, he gave a lot of big barbecue dinners. He would kill a calf or two and cook them outside. Someone would dig out a big place in the field and fix a frame over it. Then they would build a big fire in it and hang the whole calf on the frame over the fire and cook it. It would smell so good. A lot of people would come from miles around.

*****

I always loved the outdoors, and I liked to go to the field and watch my dad plow and help him when he would let me. I was so tiny I could not have helped very much.

When I was around five, this young African couple lived below us. She sure was a good cook. I would be outside playing and smell her dinner cooking. I would go to her house, get on the porch, and sit down by the door and peep in. We didn't have glass storm doors back then, just wire screen doors. She would see me and invite me inside and always give me a slice of hot corn bread with butter on it. It sure was good. Mama caught me doing that, and she told me she would whip me if I bothered that lady again. I could not stop; that bread smelled too good. So one day, I slipped down there, and when I came home, Mom said, "You have been down there again, eating that lady's supper up."

When she said that, I replied, "No, Mama, I haven't."

But she said, "I know you have because that screen wire print is all over your face." Because of that, I got my spanking. Nevertheless, the couple came to our house and played games with us, and I got more bread also.

When I was around five, I also remember wandering through a field of grown sagebrush and sage grass that reached over my head while trying to find my dad. I could hear him hollering at the mules plowing. I would keep on until I found him. I know it worried him so much, afraid I would get lost or hurt by something. I'm sorry now about that, but Mom could not keep me at the house.

I was always seeing snakes in the field, mostly little snakes. I liked to play with them. I would get myself a little stick and push them around where I wanted them to go. I wasn't afraid of them, and they weren't afraid of me. I don't know why I was never bitten by one. When I would get tired of playing with them, I'd throw my stick down and go on. I never hurt one, and one never hurt me. It would worry my dad so much. He would tell me, "One day, you will find one that doesn't want to play." I did not think so.

One evening, he sent me to drive the cows that we milked for family use up to the barn. He stood at the gate to watch me. I had to go into the edge of the woods to find them. When I got them started toward the barn, I started playing and tossing rocks. Then I saw this big black snake coiled up on the side of a bank. I took a little rock and tossed it at the snake and hit it. It sure did not want to play. In a flash, the snake came after me. That really scared me, and I started running. I ran between the cows and frightened them, and they started running, but I outran them all. I never looked back or stopped until I got to where my dad was. He said, "Where are the cows?"

"They are coming. They just couldn't keep up with me," I said.

He looked at me and started laughing. "You found one that did not want to play, didn't you?" he said. I did not say a word, then he said, "It was a black racer snake." It was a racer all right, but I pretended I outran it, but I know the cows stopped it. He got a good laugh out of it because he was glad. He wanted me to be afraid of snakes, and from then on, I really was. I have been afraid of them ever since.

My dad thought we ought to be in the field every morning when the sun was coming up. Later on that same year, when cotton picking time came, I was walking between two rows of tall cotton, and I saw this snake trying to swallow a little frog. The little frog was trying so hard to get out of the snake's mouth. I again picked up a rock and hit the snake. It scared the snake, and it turned the frog loose. But frogs could run too, you know. That frog came running down the middle, going fast. I was leading the way, followed by the frog and then the snake. For a while, neither one of us thought to move over and let the other one pass, but I finally did, and I still wonder which one won the race. I was glad to be out of it. I have never tossed another rock at a snake again.

Whenever a stray dog came to the field, I would cry and tell Dad they were hungry until he would take them to the house with us. Sometimes we would have four or five dogs. Then Dad would take them somewhere and leave them. One day, while I was working at the barn, I heard a noise under the corncrib. I lifted a plank up, and there were several pretty puppies. I picked out one and kept it. We called it Snooky. It made a beautiful shepherd dog with golden-colored hair. We kept it for several years.

I remember when we were real young, Jewell and I were nearly always together although she didn't like the outdoors like I did. We had a neighbor, and every time she saw Jewell and me together, she would always say to Jewell, "You are so beautiful." Then she would look at me and say, "You are cute." It made me feel like I was ugly, and it gave me an inferiority complex. I never thought I could do or say the right things. I felt bad around people. No one should say things like that to children. If you can't brag on both, don't brag at all. Don't tell one they are beautiful and tell one they are cute. You don't know how it will affect that child.

Jewell had malaria fever when she was real young. She was awfully sick. She was getting so much attention. I wanted to be sick also. One morning, I stayed in bed, and I told them I was real sick. The doctor came every day to check on Jewell. So he took my temperature and told me to get up out of that bed, that there was nothing wrong with me. I never did that again either.

Jewell took all the childhood diseases like mumps, whooping cough, and chicken pox. I slept with her every night, and I never got them. However, I caught the measles from one of my children. I was so sick. I'm sure glad I never had the others, but I was real anemic when I was young. My blood count was so low. Once, I was so weak I couldn't go to the mailbox to get our mail. Our mail carrier, Mr. Rainey, would wave at me from his buggy and go on. (They drove horses and buggies then.) However, I was soon in the fields again.

Before I was eight years old, I got to plow behind a big black mare for my birthday. I don't remember learning to milk a cow. I was so young. When my brothers married or left home, I was needed then to help. I liked the farm, but it was a lot of hard work.

Jewell and I had fun too. Sometimes we would walk in the fields and woods near our house and pick wildflowers. There were so many beautiful wild Sweet Williams and honeysuckle bushes, not vines. (I haven't seen any of them in years.) When we found the daisies, we would pull the petals off of some of them to see if the little boys we claimed loved us. I guess other little girls have played that game too. We also brought our mom a lot of beautiful bouquets.

When we weren't working or in school, we played a lot of games and things like that. We would get a forked stick and a little wheel and race to see who could go the longest before losing their wheel. Or we would get our stick horses and race and pretend. It was a lot of fun then. When Bill was around ten, he would take long stilts and walk around on them. He would nail several steps on them and lean them against the barn to get up on them and balance himself, and then he would walk all over the place. He was so tall. Jewell and I could not do that, but we tried a few times and had fun trying and falling.

We never went to but a few movies, and we never had a radio for a long time, and there weren't televisions then, but we did other things. Mom and Bill could make a real good show in shadows. I don't know how they did it, but it was better than some of the shows you see on TV now. My mom liked to make people laugh.

We always enjoyed when spring came, and we could pull our shoes off and put them aside and go barefoot. It was so much fun following behind Dad plowing and walking in the freshly plowed ground, then after a spring shower, wading in the warm mud and feeling it squish between your toes, then run to the creek to wash your feet or have a water fight, which was not much fun, or wasn't it?

Many times, I would step on something and hurt myself and sit down and cry. Soon it would be all right, like Jesus would say, "You're all right. Now go back to play." You know everyone needs someone to love them, and my mom had so many to care for, and I was hardly ever in the house. I'm sure Jesus watched over me many times while I followed my dad in the fields and kept me safe. I love Him so much.

I remember one night in winter. Dad was in bed asleep. Mom got his overalls and sewed across one leg so he couldn't get his foot in it. Then she dressed up in a pair of his pants and coat and pulled his hat down over her head. Now, he was a large man, and she wasn't. She was outside and started calling him. He jumped up and couldn't get his overalls on right. He came holding them up hopping through the house to see what was wrong with her, but when he got to the porch and saw her, he fell apart. She looked a lot worse than he did. We sure got a laugh out of them that night.

We had a long kitchen table with a bench behind it so all the family could eat at the same time. My mom always got up around four o'clock to get breakfast ready, in winter and summer, and all of us had to get up to eat when breakfast was ready.

We had several kerosene lamps, and we always kept one or two burning on the kitchen table every night. I remember getting up in the night, and my mom would always be sitting at the table. She was a light sleeper, or she worried and prayed a lot. If I only knew, I guess it would be both.

I recall once there had been a big snow on the ground. It was almost gone, but the ground was still frozen hard. I went up into the field with Mom to the turnip patch, and she dug up a lot of those turnips. That evening, she cooked some of the turnips for dinner, and they were delicious. She was a good cook.

*****

We moved across town to another community. We lived about one mile from the main road. Jewell and I had to go and pick up the mail. One day, when we went, Jewell got up on a nice little black mule and Dad put me up on a large mule, which was kind of wild-natured. She loved to ride, and I sure did not. We made it fine to the highway and got the mail. Then Jewell said real loud, "I believe it's going to snow." My mule must have been hard of hearing and thought she said "we are going too slow" because he started running as fast as he could. I was hanging on for dear life, and he could not shake me off, but my dad was watching us, and he pulled me off as we passed him. That mule did not stop until he got into the barn and in his stall. I would have been hurt if Dad had not been watching us. It scared me so bad I never rode again. I saw the mare throw Jewell into a brush pile, but she wasn't hurt, and she got right back on her. I should have done that, but I had no desire to ride.

We never had a swimming pool, but nearly every place we lived had a swimming hole. The kids would jump from the tree limbs into the water. That was a lot of fun. We would make us a playhouse on the creek bank, but the rain would wash it away. We also made one in the yard. We would find broken dishes and wash them and pretend they were plates. One day, Bill killed a little bird, and we dressed and cooked it. We surely didn't eat it, did we? I don't think so.

We never had a store-bought doll until our sister-in-law sent us one from California. We sure were proud of that. We would cut some of our dolls out of the Sears, Roebuck catalogue before they took it to the little house out back. Sometimes we would make corncob dolls and take the tender shuck and make hats and clothes. Sometimes my mom would make rag dolls. We did not have much time for play anyway.

I remember going to the field, stripping the tall cane we grew, cutting the tops off and taking many loads to the mill in the wagon, then watching the mule or horse walking around and around that apparatus grinding the juice from the cane. Then they would pour the juice into this long pan with a fire under it, and when it got to the other end of the pan, pretty sorghum molasses would be running out into a container. It was fascinating to me. We would go home with several gallons of good molasses to eat. I still love that good molasses.

*****

We went to the little country store often to get things for Mom. The store was about two miles from our house. In those days, they drove horses and mules and cattle down the road in droves. They did not have trucks to haul them in. I guess they shipped them to places by freight. We were always afraid of meeting a herd coming through, and we did a few times. It was kind of frightening. Men with dogs and on horses would be with them to keep them in the road. We would run out into the field to keep from being trampled.

Once, a bunch of sheep came through, and they drove them in our barn lot for a few days. I liked watching them. They looked so soft and fluffy. Then Dad bought Jewell and me a nanny goat with a little baby goat. Pretty soon, the mama got killed, and we raised the little goat. It was a real pet. It followed us all over the place. One day, we were on the inside, playing. The little goat saw us and jumped through the window, breaking a large window glass. My grandfather was furious. He made us sell her. The man who bought her promised us he would take real good care of her, but he sold her the next day.

Mama sent Jewell and me to the little country store one day, and it was wintertime and real cold. We were bundled up real good to stay warm. We had to go to the store a lot, it seems like. Our postmaster lived across the road from the schoolhouse, and he kept two big dogs on his front porch all the time, and they would bite you. There was a little young tree in the schoolyard across the road. We had to pass there going to and from the store. This day, both of those dogs went after us. We both ran and climbed up that small tree. It was leaning over so far; a dog could have been in it also. Mr. Simms finally came out to see about his dogs, but he could not call them off for laughing. I know we looked funny, but it wasn't funny for us. We were scared.

Our schoolhouse only had two rooms—one for beginners through the third grade and one for the fourth through the eighth grade. Then there were two little houses behind the schoolhouse—one for the boys and one for the girls. I also remember the boys would sometimes throw a rock or two at the girls' little house to see them run out calling for the principal. That was fun in the wintertime especially, yeah!

I will never forget my third-grade teacher. She didn't care for all of her students. The ones whom she didn't, she retained in the third grade. She made us buy a new reader, and we had to read backward about three weeks before school was out. She sent the others on to the fourth grade to get started for the next year. When school started again, our principal wanted us to try the fourth grade. Guess who knew the most.

*****

When I was around eight years old, we were in the field, thinning cotton. Dad sent me to the house after his chewing tobacco. It is a flat, sweet-smelling tobacco. I had about a mile to walk each way to the house and back to the field. My mom did not want to give it to me, but she did. She remembered when I was around four, I was aggravating my oldest sister, and she got a small black gum limb and chewed one end real soft and put a lot of snuff on it and told me to brush my teeth with it. I did, and I guess I swallowed most of it. I was awfully sick for several days, and Mom quit using snuff.

Well, I took the tobacco and started back to the field, walking real slow. It was just too tempting. I tore a corner of paper off and chewed tobacco all the way to the field. When I got there, I gave Dad his tobacco. He looked at it and then at me. He never said a word. He just called an older sister and told her to walk with me back to the house. I was feeling fine. I did not want to go to the house. I wanted to go back to work, but he made me go. About halfway to the house, I passed out. Dad told me later he believed if they had not had cold water in the field that day, I would have died. I have never smoked a cigarette in my life, and that was the last of my chewing tobacco days.

*****

Close to where we lived was a beautiful country home where this wealthy family lived. The man had a beautiful flower garden, and he worked in it most every day. Sometimes Jewell and I would walk by his house admiring his flowers. One day, he called us to come in the yard and watch him. He was an elderly man, so we went in the yard. When he got tired of working, he took us in his house to his kitchen and fixed himself a bowl of soup. He offered us one, but we refused. We were only children. Then he went into another room. He told us to not leave; he would be back soon. So we waited for him. In a few minutes, he came back. He brought us the nicest gift anyone could have ever given to us—a big Holy Bible autographed just for us. His name was Jim Stribling. We took it home, and we all read it often. I took the Bible when I married and kept it for years and years until it finally came all apart. But the memory of that precious gift will always remain in my heart.

*****

It seems like all the winters then were real cold and bad and brought a lot of rain and snow. Maybe it's because we raised so much cotton and big crops. I can remember some years we would pick over a hundred bales of cotton. Now, that is a lot of cotton.

*****

The schools would turn out in the fall for a few weeks for cotton picking, but cotton kept opening up. We would go to the field and pick cotton sometimes when there would be ice hanging on the cotton in the boll, nearly freezing it. They would build a fire sometimes, but you can't pick cotton while standing by a fire. I remember during the depression years, I had gone to the field and picked cotton with just tennis shoes on my feet to keep my feet warm. I still remember those days even though I was real young.

When the crops were gathered, the renters would start moving. It seemed like they would just swap places. Sometimes it would be so cold or raining, or there would be a big snow on the ground. None of the houses had electricity or water in them. They were all so cold. We children would explore the yards to stay as warm as we could while they put the heater up or build a fire in a fireplace to warm the house. That was so hard on children, moving so often, changing schools, and having to make new friends. It was hard on everyone really.

I can remember the first house we moved into that had electricity, telephone, and running water. It was great. We really enjoyed that, but we only stayed there a couple of years.

*****

I helped Dad cut wood and everything. One day, when I was about twelve years old, my sister and I took the wagon and team to the woods after a load of firewood. We were riding along, talking and singing when one of the mules fell into a sinkhole. Just her head and neck were out of the mud. Of course, she was hitched to the wagon and the other mule. What a scare we got. Thank the dear Lord just one of them fell in.

I ran to the house and got Dad and another mule, and we pulled her out. It was frightening, but I had a few experiences like that growing up on the farm.

*****

A few of us girls went to the Lawrence County Fair. I was the youngest one. We had just gotten there, and we were standing by this ride. An older man was standing there watching it also. It was going so slow that it looked like a good ride for children or older people. He decided to ride it and came over and asked me to ride it with him. The others told me to go on; they would wait for me. I think they felt sorry for him, and so did I. When we got on, they buckled us in. It started going real slow. After a few seconds, it started going a little faster, then faster, and it went up under a tent. If that thing had wings, it would have left that place behind.

This man had on a hat. He pulled it down over his ears as far as it would go, grabbed me, and pushed me in a corner, holding me as tight as he could. I couldn't even holler. We were both scared out of our wits. When it stopped, he got off and went staggering off like a drunk man and never said one word to me, and I was as scared as he was. I never rode that ride again. It was called the Red Devil then, a good name for it.

*****

I remember the depression although I was pretty young. I have one of those stamp books they bought sugar and stuff with. It's just a keepsake, I guess. I hope we never have to use them again. You know, we were as happy as we are now. We made it fine. God has always been with us.

*****

When I was fifteen years old, we left the farm and moved to Columbia. Two of my sisters went to work in an overall factory in Washington, D.C. They said I was too young, so I went and signed in as sixteen and went to work. I worked on children's coveralls, and I made real good wages. I did piecework. I worked several years there.

A couple of years after we moved to Columbia, Jewell met this nice young man, and after a short courtship, they got married. They moved in an apartment with his mother and dad. They had roomers and served breakfast to a lot of people.

About a year after that, Mom and Dad moved back to Ethridge, Tennessee, and Echoe and I rented rooms from our parents. We stayed about a year, then we moved back uptown closer to our work. Then Jewell and Fred bought a house and they moved. I was real lonely after Jewell married. We were always the best of friends.

Very soon I met this nice young man. He would come to the factory and walk home with his cousins. They lived across the street from us. He was visiting his uncle and aunt in Loretto, Tennessee. I really liked him, but no one knew it.

One day, he came to visit his cousins. They weren't at home when he got there, and he was sitting on the porch by himself. He could not get inside. I went over and invited him to come over and sit on the porch with us, but he said he was all right and did not come. But that night, he came over and asked me to go to prayer meeting with him, and I went. The church was at the end of the street where we lived, and we walked. He came up often after that. We walked and went to a few places together since he did not have a car. We fell in love, and he asked me to marry him. I told him I would. He went back home. He lived in Florida. He was from a very nice Christian family. We were planning to be married the following year. The last letter I got from him, he sent me some pictures. I still have them. He looked so nice.

He was very nice-looking, about two years older than me, but I never saw him again. (It hurts me to think about this part of my life.) It was about three weeks before Christmas. He sent me a nice gift, and I sent him one, but I went home the day I got his letter. I wanted to spend my three-week vacation with my family.

That very night after I got home, my brother-in-law came over to our house to see my dad about something. When he saw me, he told me his sister, Pauline, was out in the car with her fiancé. They had been dating about a year but had not set a date yet. I just wanted to meet him to see what he looked like. I had heard his brother was very good-looking. When I first found out Pauline was going with Fred, I wanted to meet him. Every time I went to Lawrenceburg, I'd ask different people if they knew Fred. I wanted to see him but didn't know anyone who knew him. So that night when my brother-in-law Odie said they were in the car, I ran out there. I had on a beautiful red crepe dress, and I was walking so fast I fell against the gate post and ripped a long piece in my waist, and when I got to the car, they would not get out. She kept saying Fred doesn't want to get out. So

I got in the front seat of the car and sat down. It was real cold that night, but it was a beautiful moonlit night.

When I got into the car, I noticed another young man was in there. It was her sister Katie's boyfriend. There was a flashlight in the seat. I picked it up and flashed it back on them. It went right into Fred's face. He made a face at me and started laughing.

Do you know what happened then? I really and truly lost my heart that night to the most wonderful man I had ever seen. I had not been introduced to him. I hardly knew his name, but I knew I loved him. I threw the flashlight down and got out of that car as fast as I could, but he got out also. Then we all went into the house. In a few minutes, Pauline went in and told Odie, her brother, we were going to get some gasoline for the car. I thought we were, and I went with them. When we got to the car, Tom, Katie's boyfriend, got into the front seat, and Fred got into the back seat. Pauline started getting in the front seat, and she told me to ride in the back with Fred. I tried to tell her that it shouldn't be like that. Too late.

We did not get any gasoline that night. He drove out into the country and parked. Tom and Pauline got out of the car and went walking up the road holding hands. Fred would not get out. Now, Fred was to be her future husband. Maybe they thought we would follow them. I don't know, but we didn't.

Fred started getting closer and closer to me, and when I moved as far as I could, he started talking. He was a ballplayer—the pitcher. He loved any kind of ball game. That night, he thought I was a real fan, but I don't know anything about baseball but football. I watch them kick the ball and run. I try to see who gets it. Then if one falls, everyone falls on top of him. I pray then he is not hurt. It scares me. Then when one finally runs to the end of the field, everyone tries to catch him. He throws the ball down, and then almost everyone is happy, and they start hugging him, and I'm glad it is over. I'm happy too. Then they go right back doing the same thing again. I go to quite a few games, and maybe someday I will learn why everyone loves the game so well.

I let him do all the talking that night. I listened, and every-thing turned out fine. He even asked me to go to a football game on

Saturday night, but when he came, Pauline was with him, and I got a headache awfully fast and didn't go.

He had to pass our house going to and from work every day. My parents only lived about three miles from his home. He would stop every evening and ask me when I was going to give him a date. I would tell him I was thinking about it, and I really was, but we were both engaged. He came over both Sundays. The second Sunday, Tom came with him.

Now, I did not know Katie's parents would not let Tom come to their house. Fred would have to pick the girls up and meet him. That is why he did not want Fred to like me.

So this Sunday, they were all in the living room, playing music and talking. Jewell and Fred were with them. I was on the porch with Dad, and Tom came out there and called me to come over to him. I went to see what he wanted. All he said to me was, "Minnie Belle, if I were you, I would never give Fred a date. He doesn't even like you. He just wants to see what kind of girl you are." He didn't know me very well. That didn't make me mad, but it sure did hurt me. I said to him, "Well, it won't take him long to find out."

The next day was Christmas Eve Day. My sister Rosa and I went to town to finish our Christmas shopping. We rode to Lawrenceburg on that little train the people called Huckley Buck. It went from Nashville to Florence, Alabama, and back in one day. There were several people who got off, and the first one I saw was Fred. He was talking to several boys. He had on a brown leather jacket, and one of his gloves was hanging from his pocket by one finger. I walked real close to him and pulled his glove out and put it in my pocket. No one noticed me. They were busy talking.

Later that day, I saw him by himself. I held up his glove, and he said, "Mine?" I said yes. He asked me where I found it, and I said, "In your pocket." He started laughing, but he did not believe me.

His sister was getting married that day. He asked me to go with him, but I didn't know any of them, and I wouldn't go, so he wouldn't go either. He rode home on that little train with us that day. Before he got off, he asked me if I'd go with him to the party they were giving her Wednesday night at his house, and I told him I would go, but I did not expect him to be by himself. When he came, he was by himself, and we did not go to the party. He took me to Lawrenceburg to a movie. When the movie was over, he took me to his house to meet his dad. His mother died when he was around two years old.

The party was over when we got there, and everyone was gone except his dad and stepmom. Now, she really liked Pauline. When she saw Fred with me, she was mad, and she exploded. We had not said one word. But his daddy liked me, and he told her to hush and never to mention that to Fred again, and she got quiet.

We did not stay very long, and about halfway home, he stopped the car and put his arms around me and kissed me and asked me if he could make me happy for the rest of our lives. I told him, "Yes, I know you could." Four weeks later, we were married. That Sunday, we walked down that railroad track, two happy kids. We were both only eighteen.

My sister Echoe went with us, and she wrote a note and signed my parents' name on it. Fred told his dad, and he went with him and got the license.

I didn't tell my parents. I was afraid they would not want me to get married. They were so hurt, unsurprisingly. I would have been hurt if my children had done that.

I kept working for a while and just went home on weekends to be with him. He got sick, and one day, I got a letter from him, and he expressed his love and need for me, and he said, "If I've ever needed you, it's now."

I quit my job that day and went home. We lived with his dad and stepmom a long time before we moved out. Fred and I both worked in the fields. We didn't have much money, but we had each other.

The first house we moved into was a little old log house with one big room and a little side room for a kitchen, with a porch all across the front of the house and a big, beautiful tree in the front yard. It had slide locks on the doors. The house was pretty nice on the inside. It did not have a well or any water close to the house. We would have to go across a field, cross over a fence, and go down into a pasture, to a well to get our water. I had to carry it most of the time because he was so late getting home. There were several cows in the pasture, and when you would go down there, every one of them would come to the well to drink. I would have to draw enough for them before I could draw any for myself, and they were always thirsty. I felt like I was the only one who gave them a drink.

We lived close to his cousin Mattie, and she was so good to me. I really don't know how I would have made it without her help. She always had a beautiful vegetable garden, and I would help her tend it, and she would give me vegetables to cook and tell me how to cook them. She told me how to cook nearly everything I cooked. It helped us an awful lot.

I worked in the fields all the time when I was growing up, and my mom couldn't teach me things a girl needs to know before she gets married.

While we were living there, there were times when we didn't have much money to buy groceries either. I guess Fred's dad thought we had money like he did, as we were working for him, but we didn't. But he was a good man, and I loved him very much.

I had bought one hundred Rhode Island Red chickens before I quit work, and they sure came in handy. The peddler came by every week, and I could sell a few and buy what we needed.

Once, we had company, and we did not have any bread for dinner. I went out in the cornfield behind our house and got a few ears of roasting corn and made a pan of delicious corn bread. I did not know how to do that. I know God gave me a miracle and helped me. He is so good to us.

We lived in sight of this big farm. It was called the country farm then. There were a lot of houses all close together. Families lived in them and worked the farm until they were able to move on. There was a big building for people who could not work or were mentally disabled to live in. I will never forget this little man who lived over there. Nearly every day, he would walk off, and he would pass our house, and every time he would get out front, he would dance and sing. I was so afraid of him. I was afraid he would come into my house. I would go up in the attic and close the door behind me, but he never did.

My neighbor was out in the yard, cutting some stove wood one day, and he saw her. He came in the yard where she was, took the axe out of her hand and cut her a pile of wood, gave the axe back to her, and went on his way. She was so scared she said she couldn't even move. She had to stand and watch him. But, after that day, neither one of us was afraid of him again. He turned out to be a precious little man to us.

One night, all the neighbor men and Fred went hunting. Their wives came and stayed with me. There was a dog that got hung in the fence below us that night and could not get loose. It sounded awful, like someone was having a dogfight. All those women were so scared they wouldn't let me leave the room, and I was the youngest one there. We were so glad when the men came back. The next morning, Fred went down in the field and got the little dog loose. He wanted to keep it, but it went on home.

We were in the edge of a tornado while we lived there, or I was. Fred and his daddy were baling hay, and the storm went around them. Fred didn't know anything about it until he got home that night. I lay on the floor and prayed until it was over. It blew our beautiful big tree across our front porch. I was so glad it didn't fall across that little house. I might not have lived through it. It did an awful lot of damage around us. We did not live there much longer.

Our baby Bertha Dee was born there. When she was about one month old, we moved. She contracted whooping cough and pneumonia and died when she was two and a half months old. She was a beautiful baby. She had black hair, and it curled. When Bertha Dee was one day old, Mom and Dad came to see us. They had my sister Rosa's little son with them. They did not know it, but Charles D. had whooping cough, and when our baby was nine days old, she took the whooping cough. She was so sick. I remember rocking her every day and night for a long time. She would cough so hard sometimes she would turn purple. I remember the night she died. A woman was holding her, and I was sitting beside her. Little Bertha Dee looked back at me. That woman said she was dying. I grabbed her in my arms, and she tried so hard to live. I cried all night that night.

We moved to a dairy out in the country. Fred worked around fourteen hours a day for four dollars a week and our apartment and milk. We only stayed there a few weeks. After Bertha Dee passed away, we moved to Columbia.

Fred went to work in a chemical plant. He started at twelve dollars a week. Our first apartment was twelve dollars a month. We bought us a car, ate good, and the Lord blessed us.

We lived close to Jewell and Fred then. I got my old job back at the factory and went to work. I worked a few years.

I already told you I was a workaholic. I worked in the fields when I was growing up, but I never learned how to cook, sew, wash and iron clothes, or clean the house. Now that we moved to Columbia, I never had my sister Mae or Fred's cousin Mattie to tell me what and how to cook. I had to do it by myself. That was the most frightening job I ever had. Fred learned to cook before I did. He worked nights, and I worked days. He left me a pretty good dinner, but for a while, I knew he ate breakfast before he came home. I was not a bit mad. I tried awfully hard, and I soon learned to fix a pretty good meal. My fried fruit pies were delicious. He even took them in his lunch. But for a while, I know Fred could have pitched a good game of baseball with one of my biscuits, and I don't believe it would have broken apart. I kept trying, and I finally learned.

I will never forget the first chocolate pie I made him. He kept begging me to bake him one, his favorite. I didn't even have a cookbook, but one day, I thought I would try to bake one crust, and all by guessing. When I got through, it looked so pretty. I was proud of myself. When he came in, I told him I had baked his favorite pie. He ate real fast that night so he could have a piece of that pie. Our neighbors came in while we were eating and sat down to talk awhile. When Fred finished eating, he got the pie. We didn't have a knife in the kitchen sharp enough to cut that crust. I was so embarrassed. Bob was watching Fred trying so hard, and he said, "Fred, do you want me to go home and get my saw and come back and help you?" Fred looked at me and grinned real big. Then he said, "No, I can make it." He picked it up and raked the filling into his plate and ate it. He knew I had tried. It was edible. I wanted to throw that pie in Bob's face, but I didn't want to waste it. That was so rude of him. I never made another chocolate pie for several years. Then I could not find a recipe he liked, and I made my own recipe. We all still use it, and it is in our church cookbook.

*****

I have a large family, and I love every one of them. My first little girl, Gwen, was very quiet like I was then, most of the time. She did not talk very much when she was young. She failed the first grade because she would not talk for the teachers. They could not persuade her to talk. We lost Bertha Dee when she was two months old to whooping cough and pneumonia. Nineteen months later, we had another little daughter.

*****

Jewell and Fred had moved out to the country in a large house, so we rented half of it and moved in with them. We all lived there about one and a half years. Our little daughter Adele was born while we lived there. She was about four months old when we moved back to town. We rented an upstairs apartment, and Fred was still working nights. It was around the first of October, and the house was cold. There was a scuttle full of coal and some kindling by the heater. I had never used coal. We always burnt wood. It was time for Fred to come home, but I didn't wait for him. I just thought it would be the same. I put in some paper, then some kindling, then some coal. I dashed some kerosene on the coal and struck a match. Before I could shut the door, *swoosh*! All that coal smoke and stuff came out all over me. About that time, Fred came home. He stood and laughed awhile before he could do anything. He said the only way he recognized me was the white of my eyes peeping through. I let him build the fire then for a while.

He always fixed the fire before he went to work so the house wouldn't get so cold. One night, about midnight, I woke up trying to jump out of the window. I had raised the window and was pushing on the screen with my face. I guess the cold air revived me. The damper had closed, and the room was full of coal smoke. You could not see your hand before you. I raised another window and fixed the damper, and soon the smoke was practically gone. I'm afraid if I had not woken up, we would have died from that smoke. I believe God sent me to the window, so I could raise it, and I was pushing against that screen wire as hard as I could. The rust was all over my face. I thank You, Jesus, for helping us.

*****

When Adele was fourteen months old, we were visiting Fred's sister, Flora; Roy; and family in Cullman, Alabama. She started having convulsions from high fever. We took her to a doctor there, but she didn't get much better, so we brought her back home the next morning and took her to our doctor. He said she had a bad case of tonsilitis and gave us a prescription to be filled for her. When we got in the car to leave, she passed out like she was dead. Fred grabbed her and ran back inside with her. They laid her on the table and covered her with ice and started working with her. I was praying for God to heal her. I felt like I could not lose another baby right now.

In a few minutes, the doctor left her and went into the waiting room to talk to my sister. We had picked her up on our way to the doctor's office. I knew in my heart what he was telling her. I stopped asking the Lord to heal her. I said, "Lord, she belongs to You now. Please let me raise her for You." Over and over I said that. In a few minutes, she got up out of that ice. Ice was falling everywhere, and she was trying to crawl off of the table. Dr. Hart sent someone to the drugstore and got her some ice cream, and she ate all of it. He kept us in his office a couple of hours, then he told Fred to go on to work and take us home. She was all right. God healed her right there. The doctor was telling my sister he had done all he could do, and her heart was already skipping beats. I praise the Lord. He still heals today.

Not long after that, we moved nine miles out in the country. We loved it out there. We bought ourselves three cows and some chickens. The milk truck picked the milk from our cows up for the cheese plant. It seemed like our chickens just multiplied. We had plenty of milk, eggs, and chickens to eat.

We lived at the edge of a big woods. There were a lot of walnut and hickory nut trees close to the house. I can still see my mother in my mind when she would visit us. She would go out to the trees and come back with as many as she could carry in her apron. We would sit down and eat a lot of walnuts and hickory nuts. I loved them.

We carried our dog, Jack, with us to our new home in the country. He loved it there. He could run and play and scare the rabbits and squirrels and birds away. We had plenty of them also. Our dog was a mixed breed—half shepherd and half spitz. He was kind of small, but he was a real guard dog and our pet. We all loved him.

My neighbor came by one day while the children and I were out in the yard. We were talking, and she reached over the fence and picked Adele up in her arms. It happened so fast. I never noticed until I looked at her, and she was looking at me so funny. I looked down at her feet, and I saw Jack. He had her leg above her ankle in his mouth. He wasn't biting her, just holding her. I reached over the fence and took Adele, and Jack jumped back over the fence and lay down. Man, she didn't do that again. Jack thought she was fixing to leave with Adele. It scared both of us.

One day, when Adele was around two years old and just walking good, I missed her, and I couldn't find her anywhere in the house, so I went looking for her outside. We had a big orchard close to the house that had overgrown weeds for several years I guess. I noticed them moving, and I ran out there, hunting her, and there she was. Jack was right behind her. The weeds were taller than they were. I am thankful I found them when I did. I know he would have stayed with her.

When I was real busy, I would let Jack stay in the house and play. One day, they were playing, and Adele came to me scratching her head with both little hands. I stopped and looked at her head and found several big lice. I picked them off and washed her head, and she went back to play. In a few minutes, here she came again. After I washed her head again, I woke Fred up and told him I was worried. He got up and looked Jack over, and he had a bunch on him. This is hard to forget. He filled a tub full of water and put a lot of turpentine in it. That is all we had to work with. Then he put Jack in the tub as long as he could hold him and when he got loose, I'll bet he ran a mile. He ran and howled for an hour or more. Poor doggie. After that, he had beautiful hair, no more fleas, lice, or ticks. I guess the turpentine killed them all.

Later on, Fred bought the kids a French harp. Adele would take that harp, sit down on the front doorstep, and play that harp as loud as she could. She couldn't play it; she just sucked in and blew hard. Jack would sit down on the step beside her. He would throw his head back and look up and howl as loud as he could. It was so terrible you would want to leave. I told her Jack was singing for her, and neither one could carry a tune.

Fred couldn't sleep, so he had to hide the harp when he wanted some sleep. I let him do that because he was the one who bought it. Adele was a little over two years old.

We also had a singing mouse there. That is what I called it. It would be in the wall behind the head of our bed, and you could not make it move or hush. One day, we were out in the yard, and we heard it under the woodpile. We moved the wood. It was a big rat. I told Fred we ought to put it in a cage and carry it around and let it sing for others. They might like to hear it. It was such a good place to live, quiet and peaceful, and we had good neighbors. We thought about buying the house, but the children and I had to be by ourselves so much.

There was a pond close to the house, and you could hear the frogs calling to each other at night—a lonely sound but soothing. You could also hear the hunters nearly every night blow that weird horn, foxhunting. We lived there about two years or maybe a little longer. I like nature's noises.

One day, I had gone out to gather eggs, and I saw this little snake coiled and lying in the driveway. My sister Echoe and her husband, Charles, were visiting with us right then. I went back inside and told her about the snake. She said, "Let's go out there and kill it and make Charles and Fred think it is still alive." I said okay, and we did. We coiled it back up like it was. When they came home and started to the barn to milk the cows, they saw the snake. Charles came running back into the house after a gun. He said, "I've got to kill that snake before it bites someone. It is a full-grown ground rattler." We were so foolish. We had been out there playing with that snake. I know the Lord protected us.

Fred and Charles took Adele to the barn one night with them to milk. Charles was holding Adele while Fred milked. Fred had just taken up using curse words. A friend of ours, Granny Ayers, had just told Fred he made the biggest mess out of cursing she had ever heard, and she wanted him to quit. This night, I think he must have been practicing because every move the cows would make, he would curse. He called them just about everything in the book. If they swished their tails at him, he would really let go. Adele could not talk very plainly, but she would make you understand what she was telling you. She was so serious. She wanted me to know her daddy had a hard time milking those cows that night. She would wave her little hands, shake her head while she was saying everything he said—every curse word, showing every move the cows made, and everything her daddy called them while he was milking. Fred was just standing there listening and grinning while his little daughter was talking like that. No, he did not spank her or tell her to hush. He just listened to himself. He never talked like that again. He quit that night.

My youngest brother, Brady, came and stayed with me to keep me from being alone so much. Fred was working the night shift. Echoe spent the weekend with us, and she went home that evening when Fred went to work. As soon as they left, Uncle Pete came to our house. That is what almost everyone called Charles. He was a very nice man, but this day, he was almost drunk. When he stopped out front, Brady said, "Let's give Uncle Pete a bowl of chili." We had chili for lunch, and it wasn't very hot. When he came in, Brady said, "Uncle Pete, do you want a bowl of chili?" He said, "Yes." So Brady went and fixed it for him. I know he must have put a lot more hot sauce in it before he brought it to him. He sat down and started eating. he would take a bite and puff and blow. Then he would pick up the bowl and blow on it, trying to cool it. It was so funny. Brady almost cried, as he was laughing so hard, and Charles started laughing too, but he ate it.

Charles had to stay the night with us, and Brady would not sleep in the room with him and his drinking. I had to make a pallet in my room for Brady. It was a new house, hardly finished, and one of the bedroom doors was just braced in so it would not fall in the room where he slept. Well, that night it came up a storm. The wind blew so hard it caused the door to fall to the floor with a bang in the room where Charles was sleeping. It woke Charles; he jumped up running all over, saying "Let me at him, let me at him." We liked to have never calmed him down. We were laughing so hard. Then he laughed with us. He was so funny that night. I will never forget. The next morning, when he left, he had forgotten the hot chili or the storm, and we never told him about them.

Charles and Echoe were separated right then. When he drank, she would leave him a few days, and they would go back to their home together.

Our first little son was born a few days later, and the doctor told me to not have any more children. I would not live to see the ones I already had grown up, but he never told me why.

Fred Allen was a precious baby. He started walking and talking and acting so much older than he was. When we had company, any children around, he wanted to be the leader. He would pull the children in his little wagon, but he would not let anyone ride on his little rocking horse. He would get on it and rock all over the room, sometimes laughing. He was so sweet. He loved his daddy more than anything in this whole world. He would cry so hard for him sometimes while he was working. It was hard to stop him sometimes.

When his daddy was home, he was a happy child. His daddy worked the third shift most of the time, and when he came home and sat down, Fred Allen would pull one shoe off at a time and drag it across the room as far as he could to keep him from leaving again. Then he would kiss him over and over again.

When Fred worked, he would sleep upstairs. Fred Allen had a little red ball. He would stand at the foot of the stairs and throw that ball against his door so hard it would bounce back down to him. He would do that until he got tired, then up the stairs he would go.

We put a gate at the bottom of the steps, but that did not help. We put boxes behind the gate; it only slowed me down.

When Fred Allen wanted to, which was often, he would climb over that gate and boxes and be upstairs on top of his daddy, laughing and jumping. Fred never scolded him or told him to stay downstairs so he could sleep. He loved that little boy so much.

Then Mule Day came the first Monday in April. We went uptown and stayed a little while. Fred carried Fred Allen around, following the bands. He wanted to hear the music.

Fred Allen took sick that evening. The doctor came and gave him some medicine, but it did not help him. We took him to the hospital, but he only got worse. It seemed like no one could help him. He passed away and was buried on Friday beside his little sister, Bertha Dee, in the Summertown Cemetery.

When he died, his daddy leaned over, and you could hear him crying almost over the whole hospital. He was with him all the time he was sick. It took us a long time to get over losing him. He was only seventeen and a half months old. God gave us a little angel for a little while, then called him back home.

A little over four months after we lost Fred Allen, we had another little son we called Wayne. I wasn't feeling very well that afternoon, and two of my sisters, Echoe and Jewell, came over to be with me because Fred worked nights then. Some of my neighbors came over also. They called the doctor out, and he told them I was okay to go on home. There would be no party tonight, so they all left except my sisters and one neighbor lady. They were laughing and talking, enjoying the Opry. You know, the Grand Ole Opry on Saturday nights in the early forties on the radio was a big thing, country music.

About seven thirty, I told them if they wanted a doctor there, they had better call one. I did not mean to frighten them, just let them know. Echoe jumped up and ran out the door to the third house, hollering, "Call the doctor. The baby is coming." That neighbor's daughter and her fiancé were out in the yard. I don't believe she ever stopped teasing Echoe about that.

Jewell took her children into another room and could not find a light switch. The children were afraid of the dark. It seemed like you could hear them crying on the other block. The neighbor lady ran up the stairway to the top and stood looking down at me, twisting her handkerchief. And to make a long story short, I delivered the baby by myself in all that bedlam. Then my neighbor came downstairs and put her handkerchief over the baby and went back up the stairsteps until the doctor came. Fred and the doctor pulled in the yard at the same time. Fred asked him why he was back so soon. He told him somebody called him and told him he had better hurry. When they came inside, the baby was waiting for them. Doctor Hart said God takes care of things like this, and he was right. He does. But I will never forget that party as he called it. Wayne was a fine, healthy baby. Praise the Lord. Everything turned out fine.

We had this saying: "Every time we move, we add a new addition to our family," and we moved around a lot. We bought a house to move into right after Wayne was born, but before we moved, Fred's brother, Wheeler, and his wife, Verba, came back from California to visit a while. They had two children almost the same age as Adele and Wayne. They stayed a couple of weeks. There wasn't a bathroom in the house where we lived, just a little house out back. Very early one morning, Verba got up and went outside to the little house without waking any of us up. Our dog, Jack, always followed me nearly everywhere I went. He probably got a glimpse of her and thought it was me going out there. He followed her and sat down in front of the door guarding me, he thought, waiting for me to come out. When Verba opened the door to leave, he saw it wasn't me, and he tried to bite her and would not let her come out. Every time she would crack the door a little, he would growl and show her his teeth.

She banged and hit the wall, but she could not wake any of us. She kept hitting the door and banging on the wall until she woke up one of our neighbors. He got up and went out to see what was wrong and helped her get back into the house.

She was so mad at our little dog. We all laughed so much, and she finally laughed also. She said she guessed he thought she was trying to steal something. After they left, we moved. We didn't like to live there at all, so we sold out pretty quickly. We wanted to rent a while longer, but we found out real quick there weren't any houses to rent, especially with children. There was a housing shortage.

We finally found a house way out in the country—a lot further from his work. The house just had a spring of water pretty close by, and Fred worked the third shift all the time then. A few days before we were supposed to move, Fred stopped at a grocery store, coming home from work one morning. He mentioned moving so far out into the country with the children, and the grocer told him he owned the beer joint about one mile from the store. He said he had just closed it down. It had got so bad and rough he made the owners of the beer joint move out. He told Fred he was renting it for a dwelling from then on, and we could rent it if Fred wanted to come out there and clean it up.

Fred took some men out there and cleaned it real good. It was a nice place—a big living room, three bedrooms, and a large kitchen. We could not have asked for more. We were so proud to get it. We lived there three and a half years.

When we first moved, I was kind of worried, it being a beer joint. However, no one tried to bother us. A few stopped in the daytime, but Fred was there.

Jewell's two children, Joyce and Jerry, came and stayed a few nights with us. Jerry played with the children, and Joyce talked to me a lot. It was like having another woman in the house to talk to.

We had another little son while we were living there we named James (Jimmy). When he was two weeks old, he had double pneumonia. That night, when he woke up, he was almost having spasms trying to get his breath. It was the first of December. There wasn't anyone at home that night but me and the two youngest children. Adele was about five and Wayne was two years old. It was dark and cold and late, and the neighbors had all gone to bed and probably asleep. We didn't have a telephone either, and our neighbor's house wasn't too close. Adele was afraid to go outside in the dark by herself. It was so dark, but I stood as close to the door as I could, and she went out far enough and hollered loud enough to wake them. Our neighbor got up and called Fred and a doctor.

The doctor came right out and gave him some medicine. Fred came home, and we sat up all night with Jimmy, and he slept well. The next morning, the doctor came back early, and he brought another doctor with him. I believe he thought the worst would happen, but when Jimmy woke up, he was fine. The other doctor asked our doctor what he gave him to break it up so fast, and he told him it was a man's dose of sulfa. The other doctor was surprised. Dr. Hurt said he had to give him something stronger than what he had. I believe the Lord healed Jimmy that night. He only weighed around six pounds with all that sulfa and pneumonia in his little body. I thank the dear Lord for watching over him. After that, he started growing and made a strong, healthy boy.

Close to our house was a patch of black-eyed Susans blooming, or weeds really (wild goldenrods I call them). They looked so pretty. I went out and gathered myself a big bouquet of them and brought them in the house. Wayne was about two years old, and there was nothing wrong with him. He was feeling fine, but before midnight, I had to call the doctor out again. He gave him some medicine, but he didn't get any better.

In a day or so, I started thinking, *Now, there wasn't anything wrong with him until I brought those flowers in the house.* So I took them outside and threw them away. Wayne started improving immediately. He was allergic to them, and I didn't know it. I never went to a weed field for a bouquet again.

Adele started to go to school while we lived there. One day, her teacher sent me a note telling me she probably would have to fail Adele because she could not read. She had memorized her whole book. If she saw a picture, she could read, but not without seeing a picture. She knew her ABCs.

That night after dinner, I sat down with her to try to teach her to read. I turned to the back of the book where the words are but no pictures. I would show her a word and help her to spell it over and over, skipping around with all the words. Pretty soon she knew all the words and how to spell them, and she could read, but somehow I could not stop. She would say, "Let's go to bed, Mama." I would say, "Just one more time." On and on we went.

It was getting kind of late. It was winter—cold, rainy, and muddy outside. All of a sudden, someone opened our front door and stepped inside, closed the door, and leaned up against it, just looking around like he was looking for someone. He was a handsome man. He had on a nice brown suit with a tan overcoat draped over one arm, a brown hat, and his shoes shined like he had never been outside. Where did he come from? The children and I stood up. They were clinging to me. I felt every hair on my arms and head stand straight up. I know we looked pitiful; we were so scared. He stood there awhile, looking around, then he said, "I'm sorry, lady." I could not say a word. In another few minutes, he said again, "I'm sorry, lady," and this time all I could say was "It is not your fault. It is mine. I thought that door was locked." Then he opened the door and left.

I ran to the door. It was glass. I could see both ways. There was no car leaving, nor did I see a man walking away in either direction. I wondered where he came from. Unless he was our guardian angel wanting me to lock the door, we were in danger.

I put the kids to bed, but I was too nervous to sleep. I stayed up until Fred came home. Not long after that, Fred was still working the second shift. The children and I were already in bed, and I remembered we had forgotten to lock the storm door in the bedroom. I heard a noise at the door. I got up and got a gun and sat down, waiting to see if someone would try to open the door. Every little bit, something would hit the door. It wasn't too long until I heard Fred's key in the lock, and he said, "What are you doing here, baby?" Then he opened the door and came in with a little white spitz puppy in his arms.

He saw the gun before I could hide it. He said he was afraid I would shoot him some night, thinking he was breaking in, but I'm sure I wouldn't have done that.

We sure did like to live there. There was a big creek behind the house where the bedrooms were. At night, you could hear the water bubbling over the rocks. It was so easy to go to sleep.

When Jimmy was about eight months old, we bought another house and moved closer to town. The house we bought was a log house on a big lot with a lot of trees and a hedge of iris around it. It was a good place for the children to play. I have told you I was raised in the country with woodburning stoves and kerosene lamps and also about building the fire in the heater with coal. Now it's electricity. I did not know what that little black box on the wall was for. Fred always took care of those things.

Well, one day, our refrigerator cord just dropped off at the wall socket. The plug was still in the socket. Jimmy was just beginning to walk, and I was afraid he would notice it. Children are like that. They are into everything, so I thought I would take the plug out. I reached down to get ahold of it, but before I could get a grip on it—*wham*. I hit the other wall across the room, with a little less hair and tingling all over. I sat there awhile. I left that job for Fred.

When he came home, he laughed at me again, then he fixed it. Why are men smarter than women at some things? I know he worked hard to keep me alive. I learned that little black box on the wall was very important.

We had been living there about a year when Fred and Jewell's husband, Fred, went into partnership and bought a grocery store. They did real good. Echoe's husband's mother lived next door to us. One Sunday, she had given Fred a big order for groceries to bring home for her. That day, her son, Harold, came over to spend the day with her. She told him I lived next door, and he came over to see me. He stayed an hour or so with me and the children. We grew up together as neighbors. I had not seen him in years, and I was really glad to see him. We talked about growing up and our married life and our children.

When Fred came home that night I told him all about it. He was so jealous he took her groceries back to the store and put them back on the shelf. The next morning, she had to come over and borrow some things for breakfast. She thought he had forgotten to bring them, but he brought them back the next day.

Neither one liked keeping the store, and they sold it. Fred went back to Monsanto. Both of them were on the Monsanto ball team.

Echoe and Charles stayed with us a lot. They did not have any children, and they spoiled our kids terribly. One day, Echoe and Charles were next door at his mother's house, and Wayne was with them. They were wrestling and playing. Wayne thought Charles was hurting Echoe. He went home and got Fred's shotgun and dragged it across that big yard to their house and told Uncle Pete he was going to shoot him. The gun was unloaded and apart, but I don't know how he got it anyway. He was just about four years old. I wasn't home. Charles said that was the funniest sight, but he said he told him he sure was glad he didn't find a shell. Wayne didn't know the difference. They were laughing about it when I came home that day.

That was a real bad move we made when we moved there. Very soon it changed our lives a lot.

Our house was close to his best friend. He was a mechanic and had his own shop. After we moved there, Fred started working for him on his days off from his job. Very soon, they started going to all the ball games and to Nashville every Sunday to a game, or so they said. I did not mind the ball games so much. But when he started coming home late at night, I soon found out about his best friend. He had too many friends.

One day, Charles came by to see the children and me, how we were doing, and to talk to me. He was more like a brother to me. While we were talking, he started just like he was talking to a friend about a friend. He said, "I saw Fred in town today with another woman. They were in the car together."

Echoe knew it all the time, but she would not tell me. It hurt me so bad. We had children, and I was six months pregnant again. My heart just broke in pieces and fell around my feet. I looked at my children playing and said my children would never hear about this. They loved their daddy too much, and I did too.

His friend had introduced him to a married lady with children. Her husband was in the service. We belonged to church, but we did not attend church as regularly as we should have. I did not have a pastor or anyone to pray with me or to talk to, and I would not talk to my family about it. So I never told anyone.

That night, after the children were in bed asleep, I was on my knees praying for my family, and I met the Savior—the greatest gift I ever received. When he came home that night late, I knew where he had been. I met him at the door. I loved him more than I had ever loved him because what I had heard that day helped me to seek God more, and I found Jesus. Belonging to a church is great, but meeting the Savior is everything.

It was awfully hard to go on as if nothing was wrong, but I managed. Then one night, he never came home. It was a long night. Fred and this woman had left together. He called me that day. They were in Arkansas. He said he was coming home. The truth was her husband had found out about them and had come home looking for them. I was so glad he did not find them. He came home, and we packed our clothes and left for California that night.

It was a long, lonely trip for me. I wasn't well, and it was the first time I had been so far from home. Our lives were so messed up. I loved my children dearly, and they needed both of us to love them. The children were so confused, us leaving so fast. God was the only real thing in my life.

We left our home with Echoe and Charles. We stayed one night in Albuquerque, New Mexico. A shutter banged against the window all night. I didn't sleep one wink. I still remember that shutter.

We went to his brother's house in California. They were glad we came out there. The weather was beautiful, and we all loved it there. Everything seemed to be all right again. We were going to a lot of places and having good times together. Right away, he got a good job on a big ranch, and we moved there. He was earning good wages, and everyone seemed to be happy again. But one night, he had gone out with the men. The children and I had gone to bed. We were all asleep when he came home and went to bed. Later that night, the Lord spoke to me so plainly in a dream. It seemed like He touched me and called my name and woke me up. He told me to get up and go look in Fred's hat. I jumped right out of bed and went into the kitchen. His hat was lying on the floor where he had thrown it when he came home that night. I picked it up. There was nothing in it, but I knew something was in it. I looked under the inside band, and there was a woman's picture. I knew it was her. I left it there, and I cried and prayed awhile, then I went back to bed. I never mentioned it to Fred.

The next morning, I went out and searched our car, and I found all his writing material. I never bothered his writing material either or told him I knew about it. I just prayed.

The men had a ball game that weekend, and Fred played. Mamie, his sister, and I went to the car to rest awhile. He had left his wallet in the seat. She picked it up and looked through it, and there was a larger picture of her. Mamie took a pin and punched holes in her eyes and put it back inside. I guess he thought I did it, but I didn't. Maybe I should have. I don't know.

About one week later, the Lord spoke to me again in a dream and told me to go to a post office fourteen miles away and call for his mail. I could not drive then, so I got a neighbor lady to take me. I went in and called for his mail and got two letters. I did not tell him, but the postmaster did. I read the letters. She was begging him to leave me and the children out there and come back to Tennessee to her. We never mentioned it to each other.

Well, about two weeks later, the Lord spoke to my heart again in a dream and told me to go to a post office thirty miles away and call for his mail. My neighbor took me again, and I went and called for his mail. I got two or three more letters, and the postmaster told him again. This time, she was desperate, begging him to meet her in Reno and get a quickie divorce and marry her and leave us out there. We never mentioned these things to each other.

About two weeks later, Fred was going to visit his brother. He lived about thirty miles from us, so the kids and I went with him. The menfolk were out in the yard talking, and Verba and I were in the house visiting. Her father lived with them at this time. He came through the room where we were sitting and went to his room for a while. Later he came back through to go outside. I looked up at him and stopped him. I said, "Charlie, I would be ashamed to do what you are doing." He looked at me so funny and went on out and never said a word. It hurt me so bad. I said to myself, "Why did I say that to him." I did not know anything he was doing. But he was letting that lady address her letters to him, and he would give them to Fred. That was the first ones. He gave him his mail, then he told Fred, "You know and I know that she doesn't know what we are doing, but I know that Minnie Belle does know and I will never give you another letter. But I did not know. God knows all things, and they had to quit writing.

The next morning, Fred said to me, "I know you are no witch, but how do you know everything I did?" I just looked at him and never said a word. He didn't know how many prayers I was praying for us and how I was trying to keep my children in a happy home. That meant more to me than anything else.

Very soon after that, we had another little daughter, Judith, and we call her Judy. I truly believe everything would have changed then, and we would have been happy again, if his cousin Thomas had not come out there from Missouri to visit. But when Thomas came, it wasn't long before everything fell apart again, and this time it was worse.

One day, I went to Fresno with Fred to buy all of us some new clothes. On the way there, he told me I was looking so old that if he left me, I could not get anyone else. That was wishful thinking. He was so jealous of me. That hurt me so bad. I know worry will age you. When we got to Fresno, I picked the nicest store I could find. I went in and asked for a skin specialist. He was a very nice man. I told him my problem, and he got me a night cream, a day cream, and a few other things and told me how to use all of them. He said, "Now, don't go home and put them on a shelf. Use them." And I did just that.

It took all the money I had. I know all that stuff had some help from above because in about a week, at the breakfast table, Fred said, "What have you done to your face?" He did not sound very pleased either. I thought, *What has that stuff done to me?* I jumped up and ran to a mirror. I didn't even have a laugh wrinkle, and Fred was the first to notice. I did not tell him about spending all of my money on face cream and about buying all of our clothes at Sears on credit either. The Lord has been so good to me. I love Him.

I put Judy on the bottle, and she was doing fine, but I never felt good. My problems were getting more than I could bear alone. Fred spent most of his time with Thomas, planning something I would not stop this time, I guess. One morning, after I got the older children dressed and out to play, I got on my knees beside my bed and started talking to my heavenly Father. I was telling Him all that was on my mind and all that kept happening. It was more than I could bear alone. I told Him I was leaving Fred and taking the children. The Lord was the only one I had to talk to. I had taken all I could take. I talked on and on to Him. Finally, I felt the mattress give as if someone had sat down beside me. Then I felt a hand on my head, and He spoke audibly to my heart. *I have heard all of your prayers, but now you are praying like a sinner. Tell me your problems and ask My will to be done according to My Word and trust Me and wait.*

I did what He told me to do, then I went outside and played with the children awhile. A heavy load had been lifted off of me. I could not tell anyone what had happened that morning when I was praying. That very day, when Fred came home from work, as he came in the door he said, "I have quit my job, sold the car, and everything I had time to sell. We are leaving real early in the morning for Tennessee. We will pack everything we want to keep, and Cecil, my brother-in-law, will ship it to us." We still had the big wooden box we had shipped our things in, so we packed everything we could. I even packed my sewing machine, and I still have it. I knew why we were going back, but it didn't make me nervous. I was sad. I knew God would take care of us. We left early the next morning for Missouri. We stayed there a couple of nights, then Uncle Mac and Aunt Linnie went to Tennessee with us to visit Fred's dad.

When we left Missouri, Fred was in such a big hurry to get back to Columbia. He never noticed the sign saying the bridge over the river had separated on one side two to four feet and a ferry was taking the cars over the river. So we went right on over the bridge. When we got to where it had dropped, even our purses scattered all over the car, but God took us safely across. The man from the ferry came running up there. He said he just knew we would go down into the water. There were ten of us in the car, and one was a three-week-old baby. I thank God for giving us a miracle that day. Praise His name.

When we got to Fred's daddy's house, Uncle Mac, Aunt Linnie, and their little girl got out to visit them. When we passed my parents' house, they didn't even stop. They took the children and me to my sister's house in Columbia, and they went on uptown. Both of my sisters fussed on me for coming back. They said, "You know you will never see him again." I never said one word. I was trusting God to do His will whichever way it went. I knew He would take care of us. I had already worried too much.

I still loved him dearly, and he was my children's father, and they loved him. He was gone to town maybe a little over an hour, and they came back. He was wearing dark shaded glasses. He said he got them when he got uptown so no one would recognize him. He had a lot of friends in Columbia. He told me he talked to his friend to find out how things were, and he told him. While that lady was writing to him to separate us, she was going with another married man and separated that family, and now she was going with another married man. Her husband had been back, but I don't know what had happened to them. I just know Fred never saw or heard from her again.

Fred and Thomas went back to Missouri that day. All this happened in less than six months. In a week, Fred came back after us. He had bought a restaurant with a service station and rented us an apartment in town. His brother Wheeler and his family came back from California and took over the service station. They kept it about two years, then sold it and went back to California. We stayed for almost two years after they left.

As the saying went, yes, every time we move, I got pregnant. Well, thirteen months after Judy was born, we had another little son, Robert. When he was born, this doctor told me again, "Don't have any more children. You won't live to see the ones you have grow up." He was the second doctor to tell me that. I still did not listen.

The morning Robert was to make his arrival, I woke up with a terrible toothache. I dressed the kids and myself and started walking the three miles to town. We had moved to the country. One of my neighbors stopped and picked us up so we would not have so far to walk. It was real hot that day. The dentist closed at twelve o'clock on Saturdays, so I rushed and put the children in the movies and hurried over to the dentist office. He was closing his door when I got there. I pushed around him and went in and sat down in the chair. When he came in, he asked me, "When is it due?"

"Today, I replied
"I won't pull it."
"I'll sit here until you do."
He looked at his nurse and said, "What can I do?"
She started laughing and said, "I don't know."
He asked me who my doctor was, and I told him it was Doctor Williams, right below him. He left the room. I guess he called him because he came back with a needle. I guess he killed the nerve. It quit hurting, and he told me to go straight down to that doctor's office, and I did. He put me to bed and called Fred. Fred did not know I was uptown. He came and took me home.

Robert was born at home almost three hours later. I was sorry I frightened my neighbor and my doctor like that, but I did. My neighbor said he wouldn't have picked us up if he had known he was supposed to arrive that day. Everything turned out fine, and we had a fine baby boy.

We were happy in Missouri for a while, not that I dislike Missouri. The restaurant kept us from going any place together. We stayed open every night until twelve o'clock and longer sometimes. Fred did not get home until late every night, and we didn't have much time together. I did not like that, and our happiness did not last very long.

He had bought the restaurant from his cousin, Thomas. He was single, and at that time, he drank heavily. He thought Fred ought to be able to go and do everything that he did. That is why he wanted him to move to Missouri. I started working some. I felt like no one wanted me to be there and soon I discovered why. Married men were meeting their dates in there. That soon stopped. They told Fred I was telling their wives. I did not know them or their wives either. I hope I did stop one man.

I was dressing to go to work one morning when this little boy came in to play with our little boys. He came up to me and said so sweetly, "My name is Wayne, and today is my birthday. My mama is baking me a cake." He held his little hand up and said, "I'm five years old." I walked to work that morning, and when I passed their house, his mom was at the woodpile getting wood. I thought to bake Wayne's birthday cake. When I got to work, I went through the front that morning. The first man I saw was little Wayne's daddy with another woman. They had ordered plate lunches, laughing and talking. I went in the kitchen and told them I wanted to take their lunch to them. I did. I set her plate down in front of her. I looked at him and said very kindly, "Today is little Wayne's birthday. Will you please tell him happy birthday for me?"

He jumped up and ran out of the building. I didn't get to set his plate down. Fred was angry at me. He said I was running the customers off. I said if that was the only kind we had, I would hope I ran them all off, but it wasn't. When we sold out, it was a family restaurant with the best food in town. The merchants wanted me to keep it and run it. They promised me their parties and meetings, but I was more concerned for my family.

One day, I was working in the house when I heard glass breaking. I ran outside to check on the children. All the little boys had gone out and picked up a lot of drink bottles and had sat down to break them. When I ran out there, just as I got to them, our little Jimmy stuck his forefinger in the neck of a Coke bottle and hit the rock hard enough to break the bottle all to pieces, and it cut his finger all to pieces. Fred just happened to drive up right then, and he grabbed him up, and I wrapped a towel around his hand, and he took him to a doctor. The doctor wanted to finish cutting his finger off, but Fred would not let him, so he did the best he could. It healed up nicely, but it was years before the feeling came back into it.

Our restaurant stayed open late at night, and a lot of people came in to eat before going home after they quit work. I guess that is how he started again. No one had to tell me this time. Fred started drinking and staying gone a lot. He would not let us see him drinking, or he tried to hide it from us. But I knew. The children were older, and it was harder to keep things from them, but I did the best I could. I had prayed so hard for us, and now I was going through this same thing again. It was so much harder this time.

I could have left him, but we loved him, and I knew he loved us too. I worked all I could, but Robert was young, and I had to stay at home a lot also. I recall once when he hadn't been at home for a couple of days. We were completely out of food, and I never had any money at home or a telephone. I kept sending the children outside to play, praying he would come home, but he didn't come. Every time they came in, I would give them a drink of water and tell them to go and play with their little friends. Children love to play outside, but it was getting late, and the other children were going inside to eat and stay inside.

Jimmy came in. Now he was four years old. He lay his little head in my lap and started crying and saying, "Mama, I'm hungry." The older ones had not said anything. Then Adele said, "Mama, look in that big black purse on the shelf and see if there is any money in it." It was a big binder we kept important papers in. I knew there wasn't any money in it, but I got it down to please her, and when I opened it, there was enough money to buy all the food we could eat and more. I can still see Adele and Wayne running to the little store. In times like this, there was enough money in that purse to buy all the food we could eat.

Fred never knew about that until just before Adele married. At the dinner table one night, she said, "Mama, I wonder what happened to that purse that always had money in it when we needed it."

"I guess we left it one of the times when we moved so fast," I replied.

"Adele, what are you talking about?" Fred said.

"Oh, Daddy, I was just thinking," Adele said.

We couldn't tell him. It would have hurt him so bad. God knew our need. He is always near. I praise His holy name.

When I worked, I kept plenty of food at home. I brought it from the restaurant, but I couldn't work all the time. Fred told the store owner to let us have anything we wanted. I guess Jimmy told him he got hungry. I never kept much food at home to cook. When I was working and Fred wasn't there to take me home, Wheeler would come in and get my stuff and put it in Mr. Hendy's cab, and when we would start home, he would start on me. "Why don't you leave Fred and take those kids and go back to Tennessee?" I got tired of hearing that.

There was an attorney. He would come over every day and run a cab after he closed his office until quitting time. The cab business got their calls at our restaurant. I had been to his office a few times for advice. I asked him one day if he would take me home. He said he would be glad to. So I started taking my things out of Mr. Hendy's cab and putting them in Edd's cab. Wheeler, Fred's brother, did not like that, so he told Fred.

One night, I had just cleared the register, and we were fixing to leave. Fred came in. He bawled poor Edd out for taking me home and told him he had better never take me home again. He just stood and took it. Edd never said one word. The very next night, Fred wasn't there to take me home, and Edd was still waiting. He knew I had to have a ride home. After I finished, I asked him, "Are you going to take me home tonight?" He said he was ready, and he took me every night that Fred wasn't there to take me. Wheeler sent a car to follow us every night. I did not know it until the last night he took me home after we sold the restaurant. Edd said to me, "Do you see that car behind us?" I said yes, and he told me about it following us. He wanted to leave it behind, but he was afraid it would hurt me. I said if I had known, I would have told him to. It really hurt me. He was my friend. He gave me some good advice. He was a good man. He was the only person I could talk to about my troubles. He understood how I felt.

Gwen married so young, and her husband drank a lot, and he was so mean to her when he was drinking. They lived in Loretta, Tennessee. She left him awhile and came to Missouri and stayed with us awhile, but at that time, things were not any better with me. That's when Fred was drinking a lot. We sold the restaurant while she was there, and we went to California for a while. We tried to get her to go with us, but she went back to him. I know she didn't enjoy her visit much. The kids all had the measles, and Judy and Robert had pneumonia with them. Judy was two years old, and Robert was one year old.

I did an awful thing. I was working one day, and Fred brought me home. There was a bottle of whiskey in the car. I took it in the house with me. Gwen was doing something in the kitchen when I went inside. I held up this bottle of whiskey and said, "I think I'll go in the bathroom and drink every drop of it." Gwen said she would too if she were me. She was just kidding, not thinking I really would. Well, I went to the bathroom, broke the seal on that not-so-little bottle of bonded whiskey, turned it up, and drank every drop of it in a few seconds. Then I went back into the kitchen where Gwen was and held up the empty bottle and said I did it. She said, "You didn't." I will never forget how she looked. There was a chair close, and I fell into it. She called Fred to come home. They walked me all night, trying to wake me. If I had gone to sleep, I know I would never have awakened. I had never drunk anything like that before, and I have never tasted it since. I didn't wake up until about ten o'clock the next morning. I know God kept me from dying and forgave me, and I forgave myself. I still can't imagine why I did that.

That had never been mentioned in my family until I started writing this. I asked Adele about it, and she said, "Yes, Mama, I remember. I cried all night, afraid you were going to die. Daddy would laugh sometimes to help me."

I met his woman friend one day. She asked me why I didn't give Fred a divorce. I told her he had never asked me for a divorce. She said, "He will tonight. I'm bringing him to your house, and I'm making him ask you. You are not woman enough to keep up with Fred. I will make his children a good mother."

"My children have a good mother, and you will never be their mother, and you can't make Fred do anything he doesn't want to do," I said very calmly.

She did bring him by our house that night. The children were in the yard playing. Wayne saw her trying to make him get out of the car. He was nine years old. He never forgot it, and he wouldn't tell me. When I started writing this, he said, "Mama I've wondered all my life why Daddy was in the car with another woman. Now I know."

After that day, she really tried hard to hurt me. For his birthday, she sent him a beautiful shirt. I took the scissors and cut it into one-inch strips, even the sleeves, and folded it back up and put it back in the box. When Fred shook it out, he bent over laughing and said, "I knew you could, but I didn't think you would ever do anything like this."

Wayne told me one day that lately he noticed I cried a lot when I didn't think anyone was around. I fasted and prayed a lot in those days.

I remember one of our trips to California. Fred forgot to put the car jack in the car. We were heavily loaded and going through the Mojave Desert. We had a flat tire. He started looking for something he could use to raise the car. He found a piece of a broken plank and an old rusty rim someone had thrown away, and he braced them under the car some way, and we all stood on the plank and raised the car high enough for him to change the wheel. I know the Lord was watching and helping us. There wasn't much traffic through there then, and we would have been stranded there with those children. I thank God He was there with us. We went to California and stayed a few weeks and came back.

We still had our apartment in Missouri. Fred was at home a lot then. He loved us regardless of things. He just forgot sometimes.

After we came back, I took the children to Tennessee and stayed awhile with my parents. One day, my sisters and I took the children and went shopping. Wayne was five years old, and Echoe had spoiled the children so much. She didn't have any children, and she bought them everything they wanted. We were trying to break the children from asking for everything they wanted. Wayne wanted something, and I would not let him tell Echoe. So when we started to leave and cross over the Main Street in Columbia, he got on his hands and knees and walked all across the street. We went on across. A policeman was watching him to make sure he was safe. He never did anything like that again.

Then Judy got pneumonia, and we could not get her fever down. I had to call Fred. He had just had a bad wreck and almost totaled the car, but he wasn't hurt. He took the car out of the shop and wired the doors shut so he could come down there to see her. The children cried when they saw the car but was glad their daddy wasn't hurt. When he got the car fixed, he came after us. Very soon after that, we went to spend the weekend with his uncle and aunt in the country. We all liked to visit them. They were such nice people, and they had a little girl Adele's age whom Adele liked to play with. We went on a Friday, and Friday night, Fred and Thomas went out and were real late getting in. We were all asleep. They got up and left Saturday morning before any of us woke up. I never saw him all weekend.

I do not believe I have ever seen it rain so hard as it was raining that Saturday morning when we got up. Raindrops were bouncing on the ground as they fell. It rained all day and all night long. It was a long, lonely day for me.

Aunt Linnie cooked us a real good breakfast, but she never cooked but twice a day unless they were working, and they did not snack either, and I liked to snack, and I got hungry. This was about four o'clock that afternoon, when Aunt Linnie and I were sitting in the kitchen with the door open, watching the rain. There was a big fire in the range, and she had two of her delicious homemade mincemeat pies with a pan of corn bread in the oven, baking and smelling so good. She said she had made one of the pies just for me. I loved them so well; they were scrumptious. She also had vegetables on top of the range cooking.

I was so hungry my stomach was talking to me. I had not heard from Fred all day, and I was lonely and worried. All of a sudden, I heard the Lord speaking to me in my heart, *Fast and pray*. I said, *Lord, I'm at someone else's house, and I am so hungry*. In a few seconds, I heard it again. *Fast and pray*. I got up and walked out of the kitchen. I never said a word to Aunt Linnie. Uncle Mac was in the living room watching the children play. I asked him if he would watch the children for me and let me go to bed. I was sick. I knew that was the only way that I could fast. He said yes, he would watch them for me to go to bed. I went to bed and cried and prayed a long time. Then I finally went to sleep.

About midnight, I was awakened by cold water dripping on my face. When I opened my eyes, I saw it was dripping from Fred's hat. He was trying to wake me up, and he was saying, "I didn't know I loved you so much." I opened my eyes to see who he was talking to.

It had been a long time since I had heard those words, and sometimes I wondered if I ever would hear them again.

When he saw I was awake, he told me to get up. He said, "We are leaving this town tonight." I didn't want to take the children out in this rain, but he said they were already up waiting for me. I begged him to get in bed, but he said he wanted to get as many miles away as he could from this town.

I got up and got our things together, and we bid his aunt and uncle goodbye and left. God had answered all my prayers that night. God wants us to tell Him our problems and then wait for His will to be done according to His Word.

I asked Fred why we were leaving like that, and he said he'd tell me when we put a lot of miles behind us. When we got to our apartment, all of his clothes were already packed—everything he had—sitting in the middle of the living room floor. Wayne said, "Daddy (pointing at his clothes), why are your clothes already packed?" He said it's so it wouldn't take us so long to get started. (But Wayne was remembering seeing him in the car.) We got all our clothes and everything we could get into the car, and we left Missouri this time of night, and we never went back.

After we got into another state and the children were all asleep, he told me why we left like that. He started with "I guess this will be a long night for her."

Confused, I said, "Why do you think so?"

He said they were all heavily drinking and were all fixing to leave together. He went home to get his clothes, and he got them all packed and ready to leave. When he got into the living room, God gave him a vision. He said all his children were sitting in the middle of the living room floor playing. They were so happy. The little cars were going around his feet and all over the floor. They never noticed him. He said he didn't know how long he watched them, but when he looked at his feet, he was standing beside his clothes, sober as he had ever been in his life. He said he ran out to the car and came after us, that he was fixing to leave the ones he really loved, going off with someone else. That is all he would ever tell me about that vision.

He never drank another drop of whiskey to my knowledge. He did drink a few cans of beer and then quit that, and in a few years, he was a spirit-filled Christian, worked in the Finance Department at church, and sang in the choir. There was no better Christian man you could meet than he was. I am so thankful I prayed and trusted God. My children had a wonderful daddy and a Christian home to be raised up in.

We went to California again, and this time, we stayed several years. We went to a big ranch in the San Joaquin Valley near Fresno. It was a beautiful place with hundreds of acres of cotton and grain. We loved it out there, and we were all happy again. We could see the mountains around us. He got a good job, and I worked season work most of the time. I would take the children to the field with me. They would sit and play on my cotton sack. I would pick two hundred pounds of cotton almost every day, then go home and have dinner ready when Fred came home. I liked to pick cotton, and it was so easy to pick there.

During the season, I would buy the groceries and take care of our spending money, and he would put his check in the bank. When we moved there, we had a lot of adjustments to make. There were several children there, and some of them played rough. Our children weren't used to that. We had two little boys and Fred's sister Mamie had one little boy, and there were three little boys there about the same age. They were rough. Every time our boys would go outside to play, those other three boys would run them back home, trying to fight them. Our boys would come running to me crying. I got tired of that real quick.

One morning, I went outside to see about them. A small limb had fallen from a tree. I pointed to it and asked all of them if they saw it. Then I told them the next time they come crying for me, I would pick that limb up and use it on every one of them. And I meant it. I wanted them to stand up for themselves. It wasn't five minutes, and here they came again, running home, crying for me to stop them.

I went to the door. They stopped and looked at me. They must have remembered the limb. All three of them turned around on those three little boys or little tyrants, and I have never seen little fists fly so fast. They made them three little friends in a few minutes, and all six went off playing. I don't remember them ever fighting again.

I stood and watched them. I didn't want any of them to get hurt. I knew it was mean of me, but I did not know what else to do. I went inside and laughed. It was kind of funny. Our little boys had just found their fists, and the other little boys didn't know what to do with theirs. But they didn't fight anymore. They were friends and played together.

One day, the children and I went with Fred to Hanford. Fred had to get his license plate for the car. We were gone nearly all day. While we were gone, one of our neighbors' father came to visit her. She and her father carried lunch to her husband and then ran some errands. She and her father got home about the same time as Fred, the children, and I did. However, while they were gone, those same three little boys had taken a bucket of red paint and painted her father's truck in places—over the headlights, windshield, mirror, and I don't know where else. I know she was mad, and she had a right to be mad.

She went to the shop, demanding they get that paint off his truck. One of the little boys was the foreman's son. He called and asked him who did that painting. He told him the Webb boys did it. Our boys had just gone outside to play when she came to our house, demanding they clean that paint off right away. They did not know what she was talking about and kept telling her so.

I heard her out there, fussing at them, and I went out there. Then she started on me telling me what an unfit mother I was, letting my kids do something like that. I did not know what to do, so I sent the boys to the shop to tell their daddy about it. He got it straightened out fast. We were not even at home when it happened.

Her boys tried to clean it off, but the sun had dried it. If our boys had done that, we would have had her father's truck cleaned. I felt sorry for him.

One thing I did enjoy was after we would be in bed, some of the young Spanish boys and girls would go outside and pick the guitar and sing. It was so beautiful.

One night, we had just gone to bed. Our front door opened, and here came this woman and man through our bedroom, talking as fast as they could, with their arms full of groceries. They went into the kitchen and put their groceries down. Then everything got so quiet. They had discovered they were not at home. In a few minutes, we heard paper rattling, and here they came, tiptoeing back through our bedroom. It was so funny. Fred burst out laughing. The man was trying to apologize to him. We made sure our door was locked after that.

*****

We ordered a sewing machine from Sears. Fred and the boys had gone to Mendota to pick it up. I had dressed Judy and Robert and got them out to play while I got dressed. I thought they were in the house. I was about halfway through when Judy came in and sat down. You can always tell when Judy is nervous or scared, even now. In a minute or so, she said real low, "Robert is on fire." I ran out of that house into the yard. There stood Robert with his little top burning on him. I had to unbutton it to get it off of him, and he was holding on to it, crying. He loved that little shirt. His arm and shoulder were burnt real bad. I wrapped a towel around him, and Adele ran across the road to the manager's house. Her brother and his wife were fixing to walk out the door to go home. He was a good doctor from Fresno. He did not have his bag, but they found stuff to doctor him. He was so angry at me for letting my children play with matches. I told him they were up on the wall. I did not know where else to put them.

He thought Robert would have to have skin grafted on his arm and shoulder, but they healed up nicely. I don't think he even has a scar. Thank you, dear Jesus.

What happened was Judy had climbed up into a chair and got a few matches, and they had gone outside to strike them. She was four, and he was three years old.

*****

One day a man came by with a little pony and a black hat, taking children's pictures. We had Wayne and Jimmy's picture made. They looked so sweet on that little pony.

*****

I made a little garden by the irrigation ditch one spring. I planted a lot of things, and it turned out real good. We ate and canned a lot of stuff from it. The little boys showed me how to water it, and they helped me sometimes.

*****

My friend Ruth's little son, Mikel, was the same age as Judy. He followed me nearly every step I made. He loved me, and I loved him too. He was no trouble at all. He would come to our house some mornings before he got his little shoes tied or his breakfast. He would nearly always have a little car in his hand. If he hadn't eaten, he would climb into a chair at the table and peck lightly on the table. I would say, "Are you hungry?" and he would shake his head, and I would fix him something. He was so pretty. I bet he made a handsome man.

*****

All the women in our neighborhood would meet at someone's house every afternoon and play games and talk. I never met with them but a few times; my children were small.

One day, I was passing by the house where they were meeting, and Mikel's mom, Ruth, saw us and wanted me to leave Mikel and Judy with her. She said she would watch them for me while I worked in my garden, so I left them. I quit early that evening, and when I passed the house, everyone was gone. I thought it was funny, everyone leaving so soon. When I got beside Ruth's house, I met her mother-in-law, Judy. That is where the meeting was, at her house. Well, she stopped me, and she was real mad. She told me my Judy had sprayed water through the window on her bed and ruined the mattress, and she wanted a new one right away. I did not know what to say, so I said I would tell Fred about it.

Ruth was in her kitchen fixing dinner and heard her talking to me like that. When she went on, Ruth came outside, and she was mad at me for taking it. She said no one saw Judy with the hose. All the children were spraying water. She said that she laid it on Judy because I wasn't there, and if I ever let her talk to me again like that, she would pick a plank up and break it over my head. Then she went in the house. I did not say anything. I just went on home.

The very next day, as I was coming from the garden, I met Judy again, at the same place by Ruth's window, and she was madder than before. She wanted that mattress now. I just listened, looking at Ruth's window, knowing she was listening. I could actually feel that plank on my head. I couldn't help myself. I looked down at that little plank, and I said, "Judy, you don't know who sprayed water on your bed, and if you ever talk to me again like this, I'm going to pick that plank up and break it over your head." She hushed and looked at me so funny and went walking off real fast. Then Ruth came out laughing, shaking her head, saying, "I didn't think you would ever say that to anyone."

"Well, I just said what you told me. I didn't want it broken over my head." I was so sorry I said that. She kept on laughing and laughing at me.

But you know, Judy became my friend after that, and when we moved, she was one of the first to visit me. I am still sorry I said that to her because I wouldn't have done that.

Fred was going to the barbershop with some other men one day. Judy cried to go with him, and he took her. He said they were going about fifty miles an hour when Judy opened the door and fell out. He said she rolled down that road like a sack of potatoes. I am so glad there wasn't a car behind them. They came back after me. We took her to a doctor. She didn't have any broken bones but a lot of knots, bruises, and scrapes. But thank the dear Lord she was soon outside playing again. She loved the outdoors. She was bad to slip away from me and go to the shop where Fred worked. She would dance and sing for them. They would give her some change, and she would come home. It took several good spankings to break her from that. It was too dangerous. Trucks and tractors were always pulling in and out over there.

When Robert was three years old, we had another little son, Charles Edwin (Eddie). The first time I went to the doctor, it was in a Fresno hospital. After he checked me, the doctor said, "Mrs. Webb, did you know you won't live very long?"

"No, now you tell me why not," I replied.

"You will soon find out." He was the third doctor to tell me that, but they would not tell me why they thought that. I would not go back to him until a few days before my time was up. I started crying one morning and could not stop. Fred took me to his office in the hospital. They would not admit me, just told us to go home and come back later.

A little red-haired intern came through where I was sitting. He stopped and asked me why I was crying so hard. I told him I did not know; I just couldn't stop. He took me into his office and took my blood pressure. It was so high. I was fixing to have a stroke, he said. He had me admitted, and a nurse sat beside me until I was better and my pressure went down.

That night, I heard a doctor say, "If her baby isn't born tonight, I'm going to wash it out tomorrow." I had never heard a doctor say that before, and it scared me. I told the nurse I did not like that doctor, and she said if I would hurry, she would get me another one while he was in surgery. I started praying hard. Right then, they brought in a little lady, almost ready to be delivered. I just knew she would get that doctor. But the Lord was good to me. Very shortly, I called the nurse and asked her to let me wear her watch for a while. I was counting time, but she didn't know. In a few minutes, I called her and gave her watch back to her and told her to get me that doctor. She said, "Webb, you can't be." I said yes. She checked me, and they barely got me to the delivery room, and the doctor they sent up was that nice little red-haired doctor who had admitted me. When Eddie was born, he had the prettiest red curly hair I had ever seen. The nurses asked me where he got his red hair. I told them I was so proud when I saw that nice little red-haired doctor they sent up that Eddie's hair turned red. They got a good laugh, and I got teased a lot. But it was normal. Fred's hair was reddish auburn, and his mother had pretty red curly hair. I don't remember telling them differently, though.

Fred wanted me to learn how to drive so I could bring his lunch to him in the field every day so he could have a warm lunch. My teaching was twelve miles and him helping me, and I had to drive in the fields in all that sand. I buried the wheels once, but he got it out. I sure remember the first day I took it to the field. Robert had cried, telling me to hurry and go all morning, and when I got it fixed ready to leave, he got quiet. We all got in the car and left. When we got to the field, Judy said, "Mama, we left Robert at home." That was before Eddie was born. I was so nervous. I had to turn around and go back after him.

When I got back to the house, a neighbor had a ladder at a window, fixing to go in after him. He was crying so hard. I never did that again. I counted heads before I left. He begged me so hard to hurry, and then I forgot him. It sure did hurt me. Pretty soon, I started fixing lunch for all of us, and we had a picnic in the field every day. We all enjoyed that.

Sometimes one of my friends would take her husband's lunch to the field and ride with me. There usually were two narrow planks to drive across the irrigation ditch on. She was always afraid I would miss one. I told her where I looked is where I went. She was always telling and showing me which way to go. I liked to tease her and make her laugh. I was a pretty good driver.

The kids and I were walking in the field one day, and I walked right into a bunch of pheasants. They flew up in front of me. It scared me so bad. I bet I ran a mile before I could stop. Jimmy still laughs about that. He asked me lately if I could still run that fast. I told him yes, if I got that scared again. No, I am sure I could not. Too much water has run under the bridge since then.

I was also afraid of those coyotes we would see and hear. The men would blow smoke in the place where they stayed and would kill them as they ran out. I saw several on fences to scare them away.

Every year, when cotton picking time came around, I could not stay home. I took the kids and went even when they were on the bottle. This one year I'm thinking about, I had a problem those first few days. I was picking on two rows of cotton, and Robert was real young, and he was picking on one of my rows. He had learned some Spanish from some of the children or neighbors. He was really picking and singing that Spanish song. A woman and man had rows beside me. She rose, listening to him; he was just a little child. She turned to her husband and said, "Can't he say that plainly?" He said yes, and they started laughing. I rose and asked her would she please tell me what he was saying. She shook her head and said, "Oh, I can't tell you." He soon forgot it.

Now it's my turn. When I got my sack about half-full, I could not even drag it. I didn't know what to do. There was a young Spanish boy. He looked about twenty. I had noticed him watching me. He dropped his sack, came over and got my sack, weighed and emptied it, and brought it back to me with my money. He did that for two or three days, then I could handle it myself. He never said one word to me. All through cotton picking, I noticed him watching me. Later, we changed fields.

The people I rode over with left real early. It was nearly quitting time, and I lacked a little, having my row out. I rose, and I saw this young man and a few others standing beside his car, and he was looking toward me. I said to myself, "He is going to ask me to ride home with them. Here he comes." The first time he had ever talked to me, he asked me if I had a ride home. I told him yes, I was riding with the man and his wife who weighed the cotton, and I thanked him. I really appreciated his concern. I was a long distance from home, so I thought I had better tell Fred about him. There were two or three hundred pickers I guess.

That night, I started telling him about this nice young Spanish boy who had watched and helped me the whole cotton picking season. I told him about all the things he did for me, trying not to make him mad for not telling him before.

"He carried your sack for you, emptied it a few days," he said.

"Yes," I replied.

"He would see you had a ride home, and he would see that no one bothered you."

"Yes."

Then he started laughing and said, "I know all about it. He works at the shop with me, and he was watching you for me."

"Yes, and I guess you were paying him plenty for his kindness." I knew he wasn't worried about me being out there picking with so many people. I had a nice bodyguard and did not know it.

*****

Once, when we went to the Yosemite Park, the children had their picture made petting the deer. They were so gentle. It was a beautiful place—those large trees and the waterfalls and so many beautiful things to see. We went to a lot of places and saw some beautiful things while we lived there. We loved living in California.

I had taken Adele to Kerman one day. All the children were with me. On our way home, we ran into several stallions that had broken out of a pasture. They were coming down the road straight toward us. I had nowhere to go but to stop. There was a canal ditch on one side and a tall thick hedge on the other side between the roads. Just before they got to the car, all of them stopped and turned, running the other way except one. It stopped right in front of the car, turned and raised his feet up in the air, and came down kicking, then he went running to catch the others. He made a big dent in the car, but it bounced out before we got home.

A car was coming down the other road, and the driver saw the horse kicking our car. He stopped and asked us if we were all right. I told him yes, we were just frightened. He said that horse could have kicked the car apart if he had wanted to, and I didn't doubt it. He sure was big enough, but I thank God he didn't.

*****

Cecil, Fred's brother-in-law, was foreman at another ranch close to us. He kept begging Fred to quit and move over there and work. Finally, he did, and we moved. We left a big nice house for a little duplex; didn't any of us like it there, and the pay was the same pay. It wasn't so nice, and we needed more room. When we moved over there, they furnished an apartment-sized butane gas stove. I had never cooked on a gas stove before, but the top was okay. A little pilot light stayed on. When I started to bake something in the oven, I turned the gas on, but nothing happened. So I closed the door and went into another room for a match. I came back and opened the door and struck the match. Boom! The oven door came flying off, and I went with it, and when I landed against another strong wall, I was sitting with the door in my lap. I can't say I wasn't shaken up and nervous. I did not know they made things like that. I did not like that stove, and I still don't like to cook on a gas stove. When Fred came home and quit laughing, *again*, he fixed the stove and helped me finish cooking dinner *again*. I already knew men were smarter, but I learned fast—just throw away your matches.

The people who lived there before us had chickens. They were fenced, and we bought them. Soon after that, a woman gave us a beautiful rooster, but we could not keep him inside the fence. One day, I was washing, and I went outside to hang some things on the clothesline, and he spurred my legs pretty bad. Someone saw him and went to the shop and told Fred. He came to the house and killed the rooster. Then he found out why she gave him away. He had spurred one of her hired hands, and he quit until she got rid of him. We sold our other chickens except one little hen we missed.

The boys had a young dog, and we had a big cat that stayed outside. Nearly every day, that little dog would lie down in the shade of the house to sleep. The cat would get between his feet, and the lit-tle hen would get as close to him as she could and put her little head under her wing, and they would sleep a long time like that. I never had a camera, so I could not get their picture. They loved each other. Then we moved away and left them.

I went to Cantua Creek one day to pick up some things we had ordered. I had Judy, Robert, and Eddie with me. I must have been driving too fast on that sandy lane when one of the children knocked my hands off of the steering wheel for a second. The car went over to one side and then over to the other side, then it darted through a barbed wire fence, missed an electric pole inches, and stopped dead still over the bank of a canal ditch. It was deep enough to bury the car. I was so scared. We sat still in the car awhile. I was praying. I just knew when I changed gears, it would roll on down into the water. I had not been driving long. I hardly know how and was in a straight shift car ten miles from home and no traffic. I knew I had to try to get home. You know, I backed that car over that bank, changed the gears as well as anybody ever could. But there is one thing I'll always believe. I didn't drive that car out by myself. I had a lot of help. Thank you, Jesus.

I broke out a headlight and a few more things, but Fred never said a word. He was glad the car stopped before it went into the water.

*****

Adele would take Jimmy to school with her sometimes to visit. He really liked that, but when he started school, he didn't like that at all. On his first day, he would not stay in his room. He would go to Adele's room and sit down in the seat with her, and she would have to take him back to his room. Finally, the teacher locked the door and took him to his seat and gave him a book. She told him to not mark it. He said he was mad, and he marked all over the front page. She saw him and came back and gave him a good spanking. He told me he liked school better after that. He just didn't want another spanking.

*****

One day, Fred came home from work over an hour late. He was kind of grinning to himself. I asked him why he was so late. He told me he and another man were cleaning out a well. The man was in the well filling the bucket, and Fred would draw it up and empty it and send it back down. The man could not get out until he pulled him out. They had worked all afternoon. Fred said that man started hollering something every time he sent the bucket down that sounded like *cinco*. He didn't know what he was saying, so he kept on working. After a while, the foreman came by and asked him why they hadn't quit. Fred was pulling the man out then, and he started hollering something to the foreman. Fred asked him what that man was saying. He was laughing, and he said, "He had been telling you the last hour it was quitting time, but you kept working." Fred learned his numbers after that. He was saying *cinco*. I laughed at him a lot, and he did too.

I did not like this ranch very much because everyone nearly drank beer. Fred drank a few cans and quit. Cecil drank a lot.

We went with Mamie and Cecil to the park one Sunday. We rented a boat and went out on the water. It was fun until Cecil started going so fast. I told them to let me out, and when he stopped, everyone got out except Sharon, their little girl, and Fred and Judy. Fred started driving then. After a while, Cecil started picking up one little girl at a time and dunking them in the water. They would scream. It scared them, and he kept doing it. I was afraid he would drop one of them in the water, and I told Mamie I was going to have their boat called in. She went and told them, and they came right in. I believe Fred was glad.

They came in. Cecil was so mad. He went straight to the car, and we had to leave. When he got in the car and sat down, he passed out. He was drunk. I didn't even know he was drinking, or I wouldn't have been in that boat with him. I believe God took care of our children.

*****

We had a new neighbor who moved in, and in a few weeks, she went to Los Angeles to visit awhile. She forgot to take her medicine with her. She called her friend and told her to go in her house and get her medicine and send it to her. She had a key to her house. She also had a big German shepherd dog tied to her front porch. It could run across the front of the house. It was a guard dog. That woman refused to go to her house with her gone. She asked all the other neighbor women and some of the men. They all refused to go in. Then she came to my house and asked me if I would get it for her. I had never met this lady or dog either. I don't know why she did not call her daughter, but she didn't. I told her I would try, so she gave me the key.

I went to her house. The dog was lying asleep. I just walked up on the porch and went inside. I got the medicine, but when I started to leave, I saw the dog walking around, and I panicked. That was the only way out. Then I started praying, "Lord, let me leave this house and that dog not even see me. I had to go home to the children." Finally, I got the nerve to try. The dog was still walking around, and he acted like I wasn't even there. He never growled or barked one time, and I thanked the Lord for hearing my prayer and helping me because the lady needed her medicine.

*****

One day, Fred came home from work real early. He had not been gone but a couple of hours, and he wasn't feeling so good. I asked him why he came home so soon. He started laughing and said another man was helping him fix a fence. They were putting in a new post. The man was holding the post steady while Fred used a sledge-hammer. He said he raised the hammer up real high to get a good hard lick at it, and the hammer fell off and hit that man on the head, knocking him out. Then the handle came down so fast it hit Fred on his head, knocking him out. A little later, the foreman came by and found both of them lying there asleep. He said he didn't know how he got them up, but he said they had done enough work for today and sent them home to rest. He told it so funnily we both laughed about it, and I hoped that the other man could laugh about it also. While I was writing, I was thinking. I wonder if that was the same man who was helping him clean out the well. If so, I believe I would have gotten myself another partner to work with.

Fred never enjoyed his meal without something sweet. I baked something almost every day for lunch and dinner. His favorite pie was chocolate. I could never find a recipe he liked—too sweet, not sweet enough. Something was always wrong with them, almost like the first pie I baked for him. One day, I sat down and wrote my own recipe. Then I baked three large chocolate pies for dinner. When he came in, I said, "Honey, I have made your favorite pies."

He laughed and said, "You know they won't be good, but I'm always glad to try one."

We ate two pies that night for dinner. He was going somewhere the next morning. He got up and made a pot of coffee. When the men came by after him, I heard him ask them to come and have coffee and pie with him. They asked him what kind of pie. He told them, and they refused. Then I heard him say "you will like this one," and they ate the whole pie. I was so happy I had finally made one he liked. I still use that recipe when I bake a chocolate pie.

*****

I got acute bronchitis and then bronchial pneumonia. It just lingered on; it seemed like I just couldn't get well.

I had symptoms of Valley fever, pleurisy in my left side. A boil came on my leg. The doctor wouldn't lance it. He said it would go into my blood stream. I had a very bad headache most of the time that I would have to move my whole body to keep from jarring my head. I coughed so much. I was going to the doctor regularly and taking medicine. It just didn't help me. I never gave up and went to bed. I would lie around and rest after I got Fred off to work and the older children to school. I still had two at home to care for.

I did the cooking and washing and everything else I could do. Adele helped me iron and all she could do. I was two months pregnant at the time and lost it from so much medicine and coughing so much. No one knew how sick I was. I tried not to complain. That is why they never knew I was so sick. This went on a long time. Then the doctor told me he had done all he could for me. He had made me an appointment with a doctor in Fresno. He told me where to go. I went back to the car and told Fred he had dismissed me, and we went home. I took all the medicine I could find that he had given me and everything else I could get. I was praying I wouldn't die out there. I wanted to be buried beside my babies. The reason I did not tell Fred that was because he had to take off from work and drive so far to take me. But I thought I would never get well again.

One Sunday, Fred had to work. I managed to cook us a good meal but not any extra, and when he came home to eat, he had his nephew with him. He was only eight years old but could eat as much as a working man anytime. I asked him why he had brought him with him because he knew I was sick. He said when he went to the truck, he was sitting in it, and he said, "Uncle Fred, I'm going home with you for lunch today."

Fred asked, "Now what would you have done?"

I said, "The same thing you did."

I told them all to eat and that I would fix me something later, and they did. I sat and talked to them while they ate. When everyone had finished eating and left the table except Sammy, there was plenty left for me. But then, Sammy took everything that was left and raked even the crumbs into his plate and ate it.

I have to be honest. I was very hurt and angry at him. When he finished eating it all, he looked across the table at me and gave me his prettiest smile and said, "Aunt Minnie Belle, I had rather eat with you as anybody. I always get to eat all I want here at your house." Imagine how I felt then. I was ashamed of my thoughts, and then I wasn't a bit hungry. I said, "Sammy, I'm glad you came home today with Uncle Fred for lunch," and I really meant it. I did love him, you know. I don't think I ate a bite that day, but I prayed a lot.

Adele usually helped Mrs. Obrist teach the Bible to the children there, but she had to iron their school clothes that Sunday afternoon and that hurt me. I had not smelled anything for months, it seemed like. When I went to bed that night, I was feeling so bad. Everything was getting worse, it seemed like, but I finally went to sleep. When I awoke the next morning, my first thought was *What do I smell?* It was a musty smell, but it did not catch my attention. I had been sick so long.

After Fred left for work and the children for school, I went out and sat down on the back steps. The warm sun made my head feel better. When I sat down, my neighbor called me and asked me how I was feeling that morning. I eased my body around like I was used to doing and said, "All right." When I said it, I realized it was the truth. My head was not hurting. I could smell. I jumped up and ran into the house and started cleaning. I got rid of that musty smell. I vacuumed and had a good meal cooked when the family came in that evening. We were all so glad and happy. Praise the Lord. He healed me that night while I was sleeping. He is a wonderful Savior.

The only earthquake I remember while we lived there was the big one that did so much damage around Bakersfield. We got the aftershock. I guess that is what it was. We were in the bed asleep. The windows rattling woke me up. I thought the boys were playing, but Fred said it was an earthquake. Then everything started to shake and rattle; the dishes sounded awful. The whole house was rocking. I jumped out of bed. Fred was telling me to lie still. He did, and he didn't get sick. I was scared, and I got sick. I saw a neighbor man run out and get into his car in his nighties. He got sick like I did. I believe I wouldn't have if I had stayed in bed. It didn't last very long but long enough. I know it must be frightening to be in one worse than that one was.

I also remember one sandstorm came while we lived there. The men were in the field working. Nearly all us women were outside that day, enjoying the beautiful day. We all had our windows open, letting the wind blow through the house.

We could see it coming toward us real fast. It looked like a whirlwind I had seen in the fields when I was a child. It was picking up sand and tumbleweeds. The closer it got, the darker it got. The air was like pure sand. You couldn't see anything. We could hear the children calling Mama and crying. I don't remember how many I brought in my house—everyone I could find. We all did that, and after it was over, all the children were safe if not at home. It came fast and left fast but long enough for sand to get into nearly everything, even our beds. We got more sand than we wanted, but the children were all safe.

Fred's daddy and Jennie Lou came out to visit us. They stayed a couple of weeks. They mostly stayed with us. That is the reason they came out there to beg Fred to move back to Tennessee. He told him his health was so bad (but he outlived Fred several years), and Fred told him we would. When I got over that bad spell of sickness I had, we started selling our stuff. We sold everything this time.

Wayne had a beautiful little dog we called Wags. We wanted to bring it back with us, but we just didn't have enough room in the car. But we did get it a good home.

It was hard for them to leave their pets and friends, but it was also hard for us to leave. We loved living out there. The weather was so nice. We moved back to Tennessee in February 1953. It was so cold and bad here. Coming back to Tennessee, we stopped in Little Rock, Arkansas, to gas and service the car. It was at night, and we thought the children were all asleep. Fred got out of the car and told me to stay inside with the kids. I did, and I never noticed anyone getting out. So when he got the gas and everything he needed, he got back in the car, and we left. We had gone several miles when Adele said, "Daddy, Wayne is not in here." We had to go several more miles before we could turn around and go back. Finally, we headed back. We were praying he was all right.

We had gone a long ways when we met a police car. They began to blink their lights. When we stopped, we saw Wayne between two policemen. He had recognized our car and told them. They had been following us. They knew we were headed toward Memphis. They said they had already notified the Memphis Police to stop us. They told Fred when we left the Little Rock station, Wayne was standing in front of it, and Fred didn't see him. He was by himself. The manager could not get him to come inside. He would just say "Daddy will be back after me." So when he had to close, he would not leave him standing out there, so he called the police. He knew we were on our way to Tennessee, so they knew where to look for us.

I thank God for a good manager to call the police instead of leaving him. When we got back to Tennessee and rested awhile, we bought a 159-acre farm with a dairy barn on it, six miles west of Lawrenceburg. We raised cotton and corn, and then we got a tobacco allotment. While we were cleaning the place up, we put up fencing practically around the whole place. We all worked hard. Then we cleaned and fixed the dairy barn and started buying cows. There was so much to do, but we managed. We all pitched in.

Right above the stock barn by the creek at this farm several years earlier, there had been a sawmill. Something happened, and it blew up, killing one or two men and injuring several.

In a few days after we moved there, a neighbor man told Fred about it, and he told him that at night, they had seen a big light and heard a man screaming. Now that would make anybody feel bad. It was still cold when we moved, and one evening, we were near this place, cutting some firewood for the heater, and it was getting late. Fred had not told me what that man said. He didn't want to worry me. I wanted to go to the house to fix dinner, and he didn't want me to leave them, so I stayed with them. He didn't want to go to the barn or anywhere by himself if it was late, so he finally told me. I knew about this accident. I was going to school with the little daughter of the man who owned the mill. We were just children. Her father was one of the men who were killed, but I never knew where it happened.

We lived there over nine years, and we never saw anything or heard anything like that. We were all over that place together and alone all hours, taking care of the cows and stock. I can't say what the neighbors saw or heard was unreal. Maybe they did see or hear something. I don't know. It was a good, quiet place to live in. I still miss it.

When we moved there, Adele was in high school. Wayne, Jimmy, and Judy started to go to David Crockett Elementary School, and Robert started the next year. Eddie was three in March the year after we moved there. I guess maybe we were happier there. We were close to our families again until we started the dairy. The dairy tied us down again. We could hardly go anywhere. We had to milk twice a day, and with all the other work we had to do, it made some long, hard days; but we liked it all right I guess. We had a bunch of pretty cows.

The farm was a pretty place. It had hills and valleys, a creek, lots of woods and beautiful trees including dogwood and redbuds. One big redbud tree was close to the house.

We bought two mules to work the farm. One was a big, beautiful mule, worked well, but for some reason she didn't like women. She would not notice us unless we were by ourselves. She ran Adele in the loft a few times and me around a tree. Adele was going to fix lunch one day, and she started running toward her as fast as she could. Wayne saw her and started hollering at her, and she stopped. We had to sell it. Fred had to put a sack over her head because I had to help him load her. I was so proud to see her go.

I gained a little weight after we moved there, and Fred called me his little Missouri mule. One day, we were working close to the house, and we heard music coming from the house. Eddie was with us. He was about four years old. We told him to go a little ways to see if he could see someone at the house—a car or somebody. He came running back as fast as he could, breathing hard. He said, "Daddy," and held his arms out straight, "there is a man down there just like Mama." We went to the house. It was some of Fred's kinfolk from Missouri to spend the weekend with us. That man Eddie said was like Mama I'll bet weighed over 275 pounds. Fred never stopped teasing me about that, but I lost a few pounds quickly.

Robert was about five years old when we moved there, and we all liked poke salad. One day, Robert and I started to the field to get some. We had a lot at the edge of the woods. We had to go across a field that was covered with real tall weeds, and they were dry. It was early spring. We were walking along, and we kept hearing something behind us. We stopped and looked back. It looked like a snake looking over the weeds at us. We said, "snakes don't do that," and we kept on walking. We had gone a long ways from the house when we heard it again. We looked again; it was the same thing, only closer to us.

Robert looked up at me and said, "Mama, I don't like poke salad," and I said, "Let's get out of here." We started running so fast it couldn't follow us. Until we got in the house, we were scared. We never went poke salad hunting again, but Fred brought us plenty in.

When we started the dairy, Wayne was twelve, and Jimmy was ten. They worked hard. The boys and I took all the work we could off of Fred because he had the main things to do. He soon went to work in Columbia at the National Carbon Plant, driving back and forth every day. We had all the milking to do when he wasn't there. He worked shift work. We fixed all the broken fences. The boys would do the heavy work, and I would use the hammer. Every time I hit my fingers instead of the nail, I would say, "Just wait 'til

Daddy comes home. I'm going to tell him something." I guess that made it hurt less. Well, one day, Jimmy told Daddy I had something to tell him. That night, at the table, Fred said, "Oh yes, Jimmy said you had something to tell me." I had forgotten about saying that. I looked at Jimmy. He was grinning real big.

"Tell him, Mama," he said.

"Tell him what?" I said.

We had fixed the fence. He wanted to hear me and Daddy quarrel I guess. I never said that again. It didn't sound right. Fred started laughing. He knew his kids.

When Fred was home, he didn't want to go anywhere without me, and one day, he had to go after a load of hay. I told him I had to wash a load of clothes and things. He said, "I'll wash a load while you straighten up the house and go with me." So I said okay. He went in and got a load and went to the wash house. I got busy. In a little while, he came in, and he said, "Honey, do you like pink sheets?"

"I don't know. I have never had any. My sheets are all white," I said.

"You do now, two of them," he said and started laughing.

I thought real fast and said, "You didn't."

"I did," he said.

I had a new red chenille bedspread lying on the bed. When he picked up the clothes, he got it also and put everything in the same washer. He wouldn't hang them on the line for me. I had a line full of pretty pink things. We all wore pink once in a while, but the spread was as red as ever.

We had an electric wringer-type washer, but we had not gotten a dryer yet. Before I got the washer, I washed everything by hand with a rubboard like my mama did. After I got through washing, sometimes the knuckles on my fingers would be bleeding from scraping them on the rubboard. Then in the wintertime, the clothes would freeze sometimes, hanging on the line. We also had to cut and bring in wood for the heater to stay warm, but those were some good and happy times.

The Robertsons lived below us. They had two little boys, and with our little boys they played together a lot. Robert liked to play

Tarzan, and he liked to be Tarzan. He fell out of a tree once and almost broke his arm, but that didn't stop him. A little later, they were at the Robertsons', playing at the edge of the woods. Robert was playing Tarzan again, probably swinging on one of those wild vines that grow through the trees, and he fell on a cement slab and cut a bad place by his eye. It left a little scar. I don't remember them getting hurt any more like that. I guess they quit playing Tarzan. I was glad. Someone could have gotten hurt worse than that.

The Lawrenceburg Church of God was having a real good revival. They were holding it in the Armory. Echoe came down to spend the weekend. She went and took Adele and Wayne and Jimmy. Adele suffered a lot with sinusitis then, and Jimmy was born with one weak eye. He had to wear glasses most all the time. They went up for prayer that night, and both of them were healed. Jimmy never wore glasses for several years and now just while he is working.

They started going regular. One night, Adele woke us. She had a toothache real bad. It was around midnight, and everything was quiet. Fred asked her if he could get her something to help her, and she said no. In just a few minutes, she was praying in the most beautiful language I had ever heard, then she went to sleep. It was hard to go back to sleep that night.

One Sunday, my brother Brady and his family from Columbia came down with a few others to visit. The men were all fixing to go fishing, and Fred was going with them. The other men were already in the car. Adele came in and said, "Daddy, you promised me you would go to church with me tonight." I didn't know that. Fred never said one word. He just walked out to the car and told them to go on; he was going to church with Adele. He told me afterward his feet felt like they had wings on them that night. They all left then, and we started milking, but I don't care how fast you try; it takes a long time to milk a lot of cows and clean up around a dairy barn. So we were late getting there.

Adele had gone on with a friend. I did not want to go in late. I asked Fred to go back home and come another time, but he said no, we were going in, and I have thanked God many times that we did. When we went in, all the young people were at the altar, praying and praising God. It was wonderful. Adele told me when she received the Holy Ghost, "Jesus was standing in front of the cross, and I knelt at his feet, and He patted me on my head" (her own words). She was a sophomore in high school.

It wasn't long after that we went to visit my parents, and we picked them up at church when the service was over. Adele looked at me and said, "Mama, I have found my church." That brought to my mind when she was fourteen months old, dying in the doctor's office, her fever so high she was in convulsions on a table covered with ice, and they were working with her. I saw the doctor leave her to talk to my sister. I knew what he was telling her. I was praying for God to heal her, then I stopped praying. I said, "Lord, I know she belongs to You now, but will You please let me raise her for You?" In a few seconds, she rose out of that ice and started crawling off of the table. Ice was falling to the floor. The doctor sent the nurse to the drugstore and got her some ice cream. She ate it. He kept us in his office a couple of hours then told us to take her home. She was all right. Praise God. I let her go to any church she wanted to go to, and I taught her all I could about God and life, and she found her church. That is where she still attends. God brought her where He wanted her to worship Him.

We were fixing to start going to church at that time, but we had spent so much on the place, trying to get started, then all the cows, so it seemed like we just didn't have money right then for new clothes. I didn't feel like I had one dress that I thought was fit to wear to church. I started talking to God. I would tell Him, "Lord, if I just had one dress to wear, I would go to church." Very soon, I got a package from my sister-in-law. She sent me a nice dress. We started to go to church. I know I wore that dress every Sunday for maybe a couple of months. I had so much to do I did not think about sewing. Now I wanted to sew, and I started. I made the girls and myself several pretty dresses, and I still sew. I thank Jesus every day.

Fred was soon baptized in the Holy Ghost. I was the last one. At night, I would hold on to Fred, afraid he would go without me. I had been saved for many years, but I also wanted what they had.

One Sunday evening, when I went down in the pasture to drive the cows up to milk, they were lying in a nice, cool, shady place beside the creek. I started praying down there, and I got sanctified down there, just me and the cows. I could hardly wait to get to church that night to pray, though. I thought you had to be in church to receive the Holy Spirit. I know better now. It is anywhere you can pray and talk to God. That night, when the altar call was made, the front was full. I pray they all got blessed. It was like a blanket came down from heaven and covered me completely. I know heaven will be a wonderful place. Very soon, Fred was working in the Finance Department at the church and singing in the choir. God blessed us.

It was raining one day. Jimmy and I were going to the barn to milk. We were both under this red raincoat. We just had spread it over our heads when this big bull came after us. I mean that bull was moving fast. We threw that coat down and headed toward the fence. We went through that barbed wire fence, went through a hedge of bushes, down a steep bank, into the road before we stopped. How we went through that barbed wire fence at the same time is still a puzzle to me. We must have been going pretty fast. Had we known about the bull, we would have gone down the road in the first place. Granddaddy Webb had brought it over and turned it loose in the pasture. But believe me, he stayed in the barn after that, or I would have stayed in the house.

Our farm was a nice place to live in the summertime, but winters were different. One barn and the dairy barn were maybe three quarters of a mile on one side of the house, and the stock barn was about one mile on the other side by the creek. We drove the cows up twice a day to milk, and it wasn't level ground. With snow or ice on the ground, it was hard to walk either way. Sometimes you would be walking in deep snow. I have had my boots nearly full of snow, driving them up, and before I could get through the barn and walk to the house, it would feel like I was walking on ice. I believe we had more snow than we do now.

After we came back to Tennessee and got the dairy and things going well and paying off, Fred's sister Mamie and her husband, Cecil, and three children from California came back to visit us.

While they were here, they decided they wanted to stay, and they wanted to go into partnership with us. We did not want them to, but they kept begging Fred until he told them they could. He was Fred's foreman in California and worked pretty well. Fred thought it would take more work off of me. I was against it. Fred was working in Columbia. That was just before Debra was born. They lived with us for a while. That put more work on me. I still worked at the barn when Fred wasn't there and had to do all the cooking.

One day, I was at the barn, and Mamie heard Eddie and her little boy crying. She went out to see about them. They had gotten into a bumblebee nest, and they were stinging them all over. She got them out and into the house. My grandson, Rayford, got stung by them also. After that, Eddie didn't want to go outside to play. One day, I told him if he would not look at them, they wouldn't bother him, and he went outside. In a few minutes, here he came running to me saying, "Mama, that bumblebee was looking straight at me." I had to laugh, but I didn't make him go back out.

Right after that, Mamie and Cecil moved to Lawrenceburg. Our little boys would have to drive the cows up every morning and be halfway through milking when Cecil and Sammy would get there. Sammy was always dressed for school. He never did one thing, and he was the same age as our boys. Cecil got to fussing on our boys every morning because they would quit and come to the house to get ready for school and he had to finish the task. I would tell Fred that Cecil would sit in the house all evening and watch television, but he didn't want to have any trouble. He was giving him half of the milk check and half of his check from work. It went on a while like that, but one morning, Cecil really bawled our boys out for not wanting to help finish milking and miss the school bus. They were telling me about it when they got to the house, and I asked Sammy, "Did your daddy talk like that to them?" He said he had said some bad things to them. Fred was working the second shift and was still in bed but not asleep, and he heard all the boys told me.

When they left for school, he got up and went to the barn. I knew he was angry. He didn't talk to the boys like that, and he didn't want anyone else doing it. So he gave Cecil one week to find a place and move, and they did. Fred let him take so much. We had to buy more cows. It was like we had to start all over again. We loved them, but we couldn't work and live together.

Adele graduated before Debra was born. At the time, we were trying to start all over again. There was no extra money to spend right then. All the girls in her class were buying them new dresses for graduation. I had made Adele a pretty little yellow taffeta dress, and she liked it real well, and she wore it once during graduation. I always tried to keep everything from the children. Every day Adele would come home and tell me about another girl's pretty dress, and she would ask me when I was going to get her a new dress. I would always say, "Don't worry, you will have the prettiest dress than any of them." I would go to bed and tell the Lord it would take a miracle for us to be able to buy her a dress. I cried myself to sleep many nights about it. I could not and would not tell her she would not have a new dress. Every day was the same until the girls had all gotten their dresses. She came in one day and said, "Mama, are you going to get me a new dress?"

"Yes, you will have the prettiest dress there." Time was running out and I just couldn't worry Fred about it. I just prayed and talked to God. About a week before she needed it, I was in the yard when the mail carrier came. He motioned for me to come to the box. He handed me a large box. I noticed it was from my brother and sister-in-law in Texas.

I ran into the house and opened the box. There before me was the most beautiful dress I had ever seen. It was white and beautiful. It was Adele's graduation gift from them, everything she needed except shoes. My sister-in-law Carmen had gone shopping, and she saw this dress in a store window. She went in to buy it, and it cost so much. She drew a picture of it and bought the material and made it herself. And she was the prettiest girl there. I know mine and Adele's guardian angels were helping her make the dress because it was a perfect fit. He is so willing to help us. She kept that dress for her wedding dress and was married in it. I praise God for hearing my prayer and giving me that miracle. He is so precious to me.

On the day our baby was born, I spent the day with Gwen. Jewell came down and spent the day also. She was living in Lawrenceburg then. She was born at eight o'clock on Saturday night. We call her Debra Karen. She weighed in at nine pounds. I wasn't able to care for her for a few days. When they brought her to my bed, she looked like a month-old baby. She was born on Wayne's birthday. He was fourteen that day.

When Jimmy was thirteen, he had a habit of watching television at night and going to sleep, leaving the television buzzing and him asleep in the chair. Fred would come in from work and have to get him awake and to bed. One night, he told him the next time he found him asleep and the television buzzing, he was going to whip him. Adele and Roy came to spend the weekend, and we were all in bed when Fred came home. There sat Jimmy asleep in the chair again. He took his belt out and gave him a few licks. When he was putting it back on, he said, "Son, I told you I was going to whip you." That woke Jimmy up, and he ran to bed. The next morning, he was laughing about it. He said, "If I hadn't waken up last night, I would have gotten a whipping." Adele told him he did. She heard him. He was just asleep and did not know it. He didn't let Fred know he was laughing about it.

When Adele graduated, she and her friend, Gayle, went to Nashville. They stayed with Gayle's brother's wife until they found a job and went to work. It wasn't very long until she met a nice Christian man and got married. They met at the church they went to. They lived in Nashville. They have four children—three daughters and one son. My oldest daughter, Gwen, was around fourteen when she married. They have three sons. They separated, and later she married a Christian man. They have one daughter and one son. They live in Columbia.

In 1957 my mother had a heart attack and died suddenly. She lived in Columbia with my sister, Echoe. She died on a Friday. We were planning to spend the weekend with them. It was about a week before Christmas.

Fred and Gwen came down after me. When we started up there, I started having chills. I thought it was nerves. I had been feeling tired so much lately. I made it all right that night and went to see my mom in the funeral home. But the next day, when I got up there, I could not go to see her. I stayed with another sister, and we watched the children so some of the others could go. Before we got home that night, my fever was so high Fred stopped at the emergency room at the Lawrenceburg Hospital. The doctor said it was my mother's death and gave me some medicine to help me through the funeral. She was buried on Sunday at the Ethridge Cemetery beside my dad. I went, but I was so sore I could not straighten up.

A neighbor stayed with me all day Monday. On Tuesday morning, when I got up to cook breakfast about four o'clock, I was standing in front of the kitchen sink, fixing to make coffee when it felt like everything inside me burst. I screamed so loud I woke everyone up. Judy was around eleven, and I went and told her to get up and get breakfast, and I went and sat down by the heater.

Fred called me to come back to bed to see if I would feel better, but when he saw how sick I was he wanted me to go to the hospital. I was burning with fever and shaking with a chill. I would not go, so he took the boys to milk after he called the doctor and Echoe to come down as quick as she could. No one had any breakfast that morning.

When he left the house, I told Judy I wanted to get dressed to go Christmas shopping. I had not bought anything for the children, and that was on my mind. My fever was so high I was mixed up. Fred had told Adele to get me two dresses for Christmas, and she had already brought them because they were spending Christmas in Short Mountain with his parents. She had helped pay for the dresses. The tags were still on them.

I loved the black dress and I told Judy to put it on me. Well, she put the black one on me over my long winter gown with long sleeves, high neck and down to the floor. The dress was short-sleeved, V-neck, and just below my knees. Get the picture?

Our pastor and several other men from Cleveland, Tennessee, were going hunting below our house. When they passed the dairy barn and saw Fred milking, they stopped and talked awhile. He told them I was sick and asked them to stop by and pray for me. It is very embarrassing to remember how I was dressed, lying across that bed when they came in. They prayed a short prayer and left.

When they got through milking, Echoe and a nephew from Michigan were there. He had come down to spend Christmas with them. I still refused to go to the doctor. My nephew picked me up and took me to the car, I guess, still dressed like that. I walked up a flight of stairs to the doctor's office. I was angry at them for making me come. I just wanted to go shopping. The doctor took me right in. I hardly knew I was alive. The nurse said, "It got you this time, didn't it, Webb?" I remember that and getting up on the table. The doctor pressed on my stomach, and I cried. I heard him say, "get her to the hospital as quick as you can." I passed out. and I don't know how I got to the hospital. When this other doctor pressed on my stomach, I remember crying again. I heard them calling Fred on the speaker, then I was gone for a long time.

They took me in surgery, and after they finished, they told Fred to call in the children and family or anyone who wanted to see me alive. They told him I had no chance to live. I don't remember any of that, but I remember when my children came in. I got a glimpse of Adele holding Wanda in her arms, and Debbie was standing by my bed, looking at me. She was two years old.

There was nothing else for nearly two weeks. They didn't have me on anything to keep me alive. They were just waiting for me to die. But God was with me. One morning, I woke up. I told the nurse my arm was hurting. The IV was going into my arm instead of the vein. I knew I had had surgery, but I did not know what for or how long I had been there. A couple of days later, they brought another patient in my room. The nurse had combed my hair, and I was lying there resting. They wouldn't let me get up.

This patient's doctor came in to check on her. I noticed he kept looking at me. I could not place him in my mind. When he was through with his patient, he came over to my bed, saying, "It is a miracle. It is a miracle." I smiled at him. He was leaning over me, and he said, "I didn't think I would ever see you alive again," and he walked out. That shocked me. When Fred came in, I told him about it and Fred told me he was the doctor they called in to help do my surgery.

Before I went home, I went to his office. I wanted to ask that doctor what was wrong with me. This is what he told me. When they started the surgery, I was in such bad shape they stopped and asked each other should they go on or stop. They didn't think I had a chance, but they did the best they could. I was pregnant in my tubes. They had abscessed and burst, my appendix had abscessed and burst, a cyst on one of my ovaries they cut off, and my kidney had stopped functioning, and gangrene infection had taken over. He said that alone could have killed me. God's precious love saved me and healed me. I thank Him for healing me and for the mercy He has shown me and all the prayers that were prayed for me. I would not be here today without them.

Fred said he slept by my bed every night. I was soon back home doing all my work at the house and at the barn again. I was strong enough to do all of my work.

When Jimmy was fourteen, with a friend the same age, he ran away from home. For several days, we didn't know what had happened to them. Then we got a card from Jimmy saying they were in Birmingham and homesick, but they went on to Florida. They were gone for quite a while. They got tired of walking so much, and they passed a house with a motorcycle in the yard for sale. They had some money, so they bought it. After they left, the man got to thinking they were so young maybe those boys had stolen that money, so he called the police and told them about it. They found them and put them in jail. They were so young and cute they put them in with the women for their protection.

The boys said the women followed every step they made. They were so good to them. The police called Fred and Mr. Slagle, and they went to Florida and got them. The man gave their money back. They had not done anything wrong really, but we were glad he called the police. It was an answer to our prayers. We were glad to have them at home.

Granddaddy Webb liked to visit us, and he came a lot. He helped us all he could though he wasn't able to do much work. He liked to eat with us also. I remember once when he came over, I fixed his favorite meal. I fixed fried chicken, creamed potatoes, milk gravy, corn and hot biscuits. He ate a big lunch. That evening, he had to go to the hospital. He almost died. He was allergic to milk, and I did not know it. It gave him a severe asthma attack, but he was soon back over again.

He came to help Fred, and I cooked him the same meal again because he loved it. When they came in to eat, I said, "Granddaddy, I have cooked your favorite meal again."

He looked at the table, then he said, "I can't eat it."

I guess he thought I was trying to kill him, but I said, "Granddaddy, you can eat every bite you want. There isn't one drop of milk in anything." I had used the potato water for everything, and it was delicious. It was worth my trouble seeing him eat.

He and Jennie Lou came over nearly every Sunday and ate lunch with us. That was the only day I didn't have to go to the barn. I had to always cook a big meal. I knew we would have company, and we always did, but we enjoyed it. Fred loved sweets, and we ate a lot. It was hard to keep any on hand since we didn't go to the store often. I made my own and my own recipes. I enjoyed cooking then. We worked hard and ate heartily. Now we eat so much junk food. We don't eat much good cooking anymore.

When Debra was three years old, we started to the field one day. The blackberries were ripe, and the birds were eating them. I said, "I wish those birds would leave those berries alone."

Debra looked up at me and said, "Mama, the birds have to eat too."

I felt so ashamed I had said that. I was thinking of my jellies and jams. You can learn from a child sometimes. I did.

When Debra was real young, she talked a lot. Eddie is five years older than her, and he wanted to talk some too. He told her one day he wished she was like a doll so he could turn her on and off. It made her a little angry. Eddie asked Roy, Adele's husband, once when they were down visiting if he would swap Wanda for Debra. He thought she would not talk so much. Eddie told me one day they were playing in the yard. She wanted something he had, and he got behind her, bumping her with his knees, and she started crying. He saw Daddy getting out from under the car, and he started running down the road, but Daddy started running also. He said he got tired and tried to hide, but Daddy came on and caught him and gave him a spanking. He probably spanked him for running from him. He said he did not know Daddy was under the car working on it.

Now I never said we never had any problems or got angry sometimes at each other, but we never had a quarrel about anything—never.

One day, Fred told me to tell the boys to fix a gate that was dragging over in the pasture when they came home from school, but when I finished my work that morning, I went and fixed it myself. When he came home from work that day, the first thing he did was take the boys to the barn and get ready to milk. He asked them if they had fixed the gate. They told him "No, Mama had already fixed it." That was the maddest I ever saw him at me. He came by the house, going to the stock barn. He opened the kitchen door far enough to stick his head in and hollered at me. "I didn't tell you to fix that gate. I told you to tell them boys to fix it." I was at the kitchen sink washing dishes, and Adele was drying them and putting them away. I grabbed a plate out of the water and slung it back and hollered "shut up." He slammed the door shut and went on. When he came back to the house, he peeped in to see if I was still washing dishes. Then he came in the house, laughing about it. He asked me if I would really have thrown that plate at him. I said I don't know, but I'm sure glad he went on. That was our biggest quarrel and Adele laughed about it. That was just before she got married.

When Wayne just turned seventeen, he joined the army, and he didn't like it at all. He was so young, and he had never been away from home. I will never forget his first leave. He came home on a Sunday. We weren't expecting him, and we were in church. When the service was over and we went outside, he was standing on the church steps. We were so glad to see him. He could stay at home a week I believe. Wayne and Jimmy spent so much time together that week. We had so much work to do we never had much time to visit, but we always did the best we could.

The time slipped by so fast, and the day came for him to leave. Fred had to work that day, so Jimmy and Wayne took the truck to take him to the bus stop. When the truck came back, I saw Wayne driving back in the yard. I was so happy to see him, but where was Jimmy? He had gone to the army in Wayne's place. He was fifteen years old. Wayne had taught him all he had learned—how to salute, to whom, and so forth. It hurt me so bad. I wondered what they would do to him when he got there, and I didn't want Wayne to go back either.

When Fred came home that evening and I told him Wayne was outside working, he started crying. I know that was the hardest thing he had ever done—telling his son he had to go back. He went on to the barn where Wayne was working, and he called our pastor. I'm sure he came out there. I know our pastor called headquarters and told them what had happened. He said that man started laughing and said there would be fun in the camp tonight. He said, "I'll meet him when he gets here." When Jimmy got to Memphis, he saw one of the big men, and he had forgotten to whom and when to salute, so he went to a phone so Wayne could tell him again. Fred answered the phone and told him to stay there until Wayne got there. He was on his way back. They did not make it hard on Wayne, but it sure was hard on all of us, and Wayne liked it better after he went back and was a military policeman. We had to get him out later on a hardship discharge when Fred had surgery to help us.

After Debra was born, my health started getting a little bad. I was always so anemic. When I was young and underweight, I took a lot of iron tablets and tonic. It helped me for several years. Then I took liver shots. Three different doctors (in Tennessee, California, and Missouri) told me I would not live to see my children grow up, but they would never tell me why they thought that. They would just say I would soon find out. It didn't bother me. Wayne helped me so much in the house and cooking while he was at home, and that helped me.

Debra was four years old when I found out my problems. I knew I was sick, but I never thought about dying. One morning, I got up to get breakfast. I got so sick I could not talk. Every time I opened my mouth to speak, I would start to vomit. Fred took me to the emergency room, and they had to admit me and put in a stomach pump and give me a shot before I could talk to them. They left it in until they found my trouble. They ran all kinds of tests and X-rays, and then they would not tell me what was wrong with me. Maybe they told Fred. I don't know. The doctor came in one morning and said, "Mrs. Webb, you don't have a pint of blood in your whole body." I knew he was teasing me, but they started giving me blood transfusions that day.

At first, I would go in for blood twice a month. I put it off as long as I could, but they kept getting closer and closer together until I could have taken one every day.

I would go home from the hospital and go to the barn and help them. I canned enough stuff for winter use and filled a big freezer out of our garden besides pickles, jellies, and jams. I took care of the house and the children, cooked, and sewed. I believe I was smart, right? No, I believe that is why I am still alive. I never gave up.

Fred did not like sandwiches, and I cooked three meals a day when he was home, and I always baked a cake, pie, or some dessert for every meal. One of my daughters asked me recently how I did that. She remembered about it. I told her you do the best you can, and I enjoyed doing it for my family.

Very shortly, I was going to the hospital every week, and the blood transfusions kept getting closer. I hated to go so bad. Debra was so used to me going. I would kiss her, and she would go right back to sleep. It went on for several months like that.

Fred had to have minor surgery, and when he went back for a checkup, I went with him. I had only been out of the hospital a few days. I went into the office with him. When the doctor came in, he asked us which one wanted to be first. I told him it wasn't for me this time. He looked at me and said, "I think you should be first." He called his nurse, and she took me to the lab to draw blood for a blood count. When she was through, I sat down by the door, waiting for Fred, but the doctor came out and went into the lab. The nurse asked him why my count was so low. I could hear every word they said, and he said she has leukemia. Then I knew why the doctors kept telling me I wouldn't live very long. I also knew I was in the last stage of it. That is why I felt so bad.

Fred was so good to me. He was fixing to sell our things and go back to California. He thought I would feel better. In a day or so, we had to go back to the hospital. They could not get my blood count up, so I had to have more blood. They would always give me a transfusion, and I could go home the next day. This time, I couldn't.

About five o'clock the next morning, the little nurse brought that bottle in and taped my arm to the plank so I couldn't move my arm. The needle was already in place, and she started the blood. I was watching as it came down that tube to my arm, and when it hit my blood, it would not mix with my blood. So quick, like something grabbed me, so quick and easy, I came out of my body. I was above my bed, looking down at myself lying there with my eyes closed like I was asleep. Then I started going over the room.

I wasn't alone. A body just like mine, only larger, was with me. We were close to the ceiling. I saw places and things in the hospital I had never seen. Then we came back to my room. The nurse had her head lying on me. I started coming down slowly. When I was about a foot above myself, I went back into my body, and when I moved, the nurse jumped up and grabbed my arm, trying to take the needle out. I laid my other hand on hers and told her to turn the blood back on. She said, "I can't do that." I said if I need it, turn it back on, and she did. It ran an hour or so or a little longer. I got so nervous. I was trying to get out of that bed. A man was coming down the hall and saw me and went and got a nurse. She came and took the needle out.

Fred came by from work that night. He told me to get up early the next morning. He would be there after me. I would never have to take another transfusion for leukemia for God healed me that day. He did not know what had happened that morning.

Early the next morning, he was up there after me. I had to wait for the doctor to dismiss me. When he came in, he said, "Mrs. Webb, we are sending you home today. We can't give you any more blood after what happened yesterday, but I might have to do surgery on you while we have you built up some. Something showed up in the X-ray."

I said, "Dr. Molloy, the Lord healed me yesterday."

He said, "I know, but I have to check you." So he did, and he found nothing, and my blood was normal. I went home that day in 1959, and I have never been told again I had low blood or leukemia. God healed me. Praise His holy name. He is a wonderful Savior. I love Him.

After Wayne left home, the two younger boys had to help run the dairy. Robert was in the seventh grade, and Eddie was in the fourth grade, about the same age the older boys were when we started. It is awfully hard for young children to work so hard like that, and we had more cows now. They did a real good job. We had one big Guernsey cow you could not get the milkers on. Eddie would milk her by hand. He was so little he could almost sit under her. She was very protective of him when the other cow beside her would prance around.

They would nearly always be through milking when time came to go and get ready for school. If not, I would finish. I always did all the washing of the equipment and wash the floors. When Fred could, he would help me.

*****

I'll never forget how Fred could not pass a hitchhiker. He would always stop and pick them up even if we were with him. He picked up a man one day. He remembered Fred. He said he was going through a couple of years before, and Fred picked him up. He would always give them some money for food. He told me one evening he had picked a woman up, and he had told her about Jesus. The following Sunday, she was in church, and he introduced me to her. He was so proud.

We went to Alabama one Sunday. Coming home, we picked up an older man. He was well dressed and very knowledgeable in the Bible. He told us many things. He wanted to go home with us, but Fred told him all the work we had to do and about how we worked. He offered to help him find a place to stay that night, but he thanked Fred and said he could find one. All of us wanted him to stay with us. He got out of the car. I wonder sometimes if he was sent to us for a reason.

While we were in Alabama, we went to the farm where I was born. The bungalow house still stood in a field. It looked awfully lonely to me. It seemed like children should have been playing around it. It was quite a distance from the highway.

We did not go to the grocery store often. We did not eat sandwiches or junk food then, but that day, we were just about out of everything to cook with—oil or seasonings. We were fixing to step out the door when our pastor and men, mostly preachers from Cleveland, Tennessee (at least two carloads), stopped for lunch. Everybody knew the first thing Fred would say—have you eaten yet? However, he wasn't the cook or the cleanup person.

We always had plenty of both kinds of potatoes because we raised them and all kinds of canned food. It didn't take me long to fix a good meal, but this day, I had to season everything with sausage fat. I had fixed a big pan of sausage for breakfast and just set the pan in the oven. It sure came in handy. When I used all that I needed to season with, I country-fried a big pan of sweet potatoes in the sausage drippings. One preacher begged me to tell him how I fixed them. He said they were the best sweet potatoes he had ever eaten. I told him he was just hungry. I couldn't because then they would know everything was seasoned with sausage. I guess I have cooked for more preachers than most women to not have been married to one. Fred and I both enjoyed seeing people eat. I did not mind it so much. I did need a little help sometimes.

*****

When Jimmy was seventeen, he joined the army. One of his friends joined with him. They promised them they could stay together, but that was not true. After they were sworn in, I don't think they ever saw each other again. Jimmy was stationed in North Carolina. He spent three years in the service. He was a paratrooper. After a while, he started calling his daddy and me to pray for them when they were fixing to jump from the plane, and we always did. They got into some tight spots sometimes.

One night, after we had gone to bed and Fred was already asleep, I got a burden to pray for Jimmy. I had to pray, and it seemed like there was no stopping. The feeling stayed with me all night, and I prayed and cried almost all night. The next morning, I told Fred about it, and he prayed for them also. That day, about two thirty, when Fred started to work, they almost ran into each other. Fred was pulling out of the driveway, and James was pulling in. I saw them in the yard talking, and Jimmy was showing him the front of his car. I went out there. He started telling us what happened on his way home from North Carolina. Then I knew why God had wanted me to pray for him all night.

The first thing he told us was he had not slept any the night before he left to come home. He had gone several miles when the gravel hitting his car woke him up. He was on the wrong side of the road, he said, and when he opened his eyes, the first thing he saw was the water. He was fixing to go down a steep embankment into the river. He barely had time to move over, but he never stopped to sleep. He kept driving. A little later, down the road, the bullhorns from one of those big trucks woke him. He was on the wrong side again, going straight into that big truck. He just barely had time to move over when it passed him. He kept driving and never stopped to sleep any.

A little farther on down the road, he said he woke up. He was driving real fast, heading straight into the side of a bridge. He did not have time to stop or move over, but he said he saw this little road right beside the bridge and took it and stopped. He said it seemed like an angel said to him then, "Son, I have you in my hands now," and he never went back to sleep. A little farther down the road, he was just driving along, and a big truck passed him with a cover over the back with some people in it, and when it passed him, someone threw a half of a cement block at his car. He thought it was coming through his windshield, but it dropped and lodged in his radiator and bumper. It would probably have killed him if it had come through the windshield. The devil tried to kill him on that trip home, but the Lord was watching over him. I praise the Lord for taking care of him.

*****

When Judy was a freshman in high school, she took Home Economics and learned how to cook. She wanted to show us what she had learned, so she baked us two apple pies, and I used large pans. We did not have time to eat dinner that night before we milked, and it hurt her feelings. So while we were milking, she ate one of those pies by herself and just left one for all of us. It was good, but not enough. She had eaten so much that she got awfully sick. She would not taste an apple pie for a few years and still doesn't like them, but I think she bakes one for her family every once in a while.

Judy played basketball in school, and she played real good. Now she works with a youth group at her church, and they can't believe how good she still plays since she is just five feet tall and a little overweight.

*****

One Sunday, Robert brought one of his friends home with him from church. He came out a lot of times, but this time, he took Eddie and his friend to a big creek below our house to swim. The creek ran from a big spring that a lot of people had their water piped into their house, including us and our dairy barn. It was nearly as cold as ice water.

When that boy jumped into the water, he jumped out faster than he jumped in. It almost took his breath away. They came to the house laughing. Our boys said they were used to it. How do you get used to playing in ice water?

*****

Several months after I was healed of leukemia, I went back to the doctor for a checkup. After a few tests were run, the doctor said, "Mrs. Webb, I hate to tell you, but you have sugar diabetes." I waited until I got home to cry. I was so mad at the devil trying to put something else on me. I know God doesn't want us to be sick all the time. I went into my room when I got home and started crying and praying. I was saying, "I don't have it, I won't accept it" over and over. The next day, they had to run more tests to see how bad I was. When the tests were over and finished, they found no sign of it. I thank God for healing me. God is so merciful to us.

*****

There was a widow who lived close to us. We would stop and pick her up and take her places with us pretty often so she could get out of the house. She loved that. One day, she took her son a drink of water to the field where he was working. While she was in the field, she started having chest pains. She wouldn't tell her son. She waited until she got home and called us. We went right to her house, and Fred got her to let him call her sons and an ambulance. They took her to the hospital. She died the next day. It was her heart. We sure did miss her. Her son was a blessing to me after Fred passed away. He came to the barn many times to help us. I don't know what I would have done sometimes without his help and the boys. Fred was always helping someone, and God sent someone to help us. Wayne came and helped me when he could. A short time after that, our lives changed so much.

On December 14, 1961, in the evening, I got my husband up to go to work. He was working the third shift that night. For some reason, he did not want to get up. I had to call him a couple of times, and most of the time, he would already be up, and I did not have to wake him. I recall that night, after he got to the car, he came back in the house and kissed me again. I did not know that would be the very last time he would ever be at home with us again. About four o'clock the next morning, I got a phone call. There had been an accident at the plant, and Fred was in the Maury County Hospital. His job that night had been placing barrels on a catwalk, and a crane would pick them up and move them where they were heated.

I don't know much about it, but they said he fell off. I will never believe it. I believe the crane accidentally knocked him off on those barrels whose sides were thin like silver dollars. That is why he was so cut and bruised all over. He had a broken leg and internal injuries.

Blood clots kept passing through his lungs, each one almost killing him.

Jimmy came home from the army to be with us. I stayed with him all I could. He was in the hospital almost three weeks. He wanted to go home so bad, and they finally told him he could go home. He was so happy. I went home that day, and the next day, I threw out our den furniture and got a hospital bed and fixed everything so he would be comfortable. Debra and I talked to him that night. He was so glad he was coming home the next day. Debbie talked to him last. He told her to take care of Mama until he got home. I thought he would be home the next day. Jimmy went back to the army that day. Wayne took him as far as Memphis just to be with him.

That very night, while the boys and I were milking in the barn, I saw myself following his casket down the church aisle. It made me so nervous, but I kept telling myself, "He is coming home in the morning." Then this strange man came into the barn. He was so nice and friendly. He said he had come to take the boys to a game or show when we finished. Normally, I would have known it would be too late for that, especially with a man I had never seen. Robert was fourteen, and Eddie was eleven. I never thought anything about it.

He stayed until we were through milking and finished, then he walked to the house with us, and he went inside. As soon as we got to the house, the phone rang. It was a nurse. She asked me if I could come to the hospital. My husband had taken a turn for the worse. Before I had time to call anyone, the phone rang again. This time, it was the doctor, and when I answered he just said we had lost him. I threw the phone down, and Robert picked it up. I don't know what he told them. I don't know how we got dressed or who took us to the hospital. The next thing I remember is being in the hospital crying.

When I had this vision at the barn, I'm sure that is when he died, and they had to wait for us to get to the house. I remember asking the children about that nice man who came to the barn and to the house with us. The boys said there was no man at the barn with us. I asked Judy if she saw him, and she said no man came to the house with us. I was the only one who saw him. It could have been an angel. I don't know, but I thank him whoever he was. He was a blessing to me.

There was a big snow on the ground, and ice covered the roads. His family had a hard time getting back. The planes were laying over. The weather was so bad, but the ones in Missouri, Alabama, and Texas drove through. We kept him out until they all got here. I was glad they all made it safe.

The church was full of people, and he had some beautiful flowers. I don't recall much that happened during that time. That was the saddest time of my life. I know a plane was waiting to bring Jimmy back home and a note telling Wayne about it. It was a shock to all of us, and that made it even harder.

I missed him so much. Nearly every time he came home, he would say just "one more day closer to my Lord." Every time I looked out the window, I could see him walking through the pasture toward the barn. When I was at the barn, after the boys would have to leave to get ready for school, I could hear his car drive up behind the barn, hear him singing or whistling, and call me to come on and go eat breakfast and we would finish later. That is what we always did.

It was so plain. Sometimes I would quit working and answer him and go to the door. He would not be there, and I would break down and start crying.

It went on like that for a couple of months. I could not take it any longer. I was so depressed. I put the farm up for sale. We had a nice place, 159 acres nearly all fenced, lots of fine cows and equipment. Like I hadn't been through enough, the auctioneer sold me out. He didn't advertise or put up any directions. The ones who did find us, he asked not to bid on anything. He told them he would get everything cheap for them, but he didn't do that either. I didn't get enough to pay for us a small house to live in. He had a friend who wanted it, a lady told me afterward. The Lord sees all things.

I could not even drive the car after he was gone. Before, I could drive the truck or tractor. Fred's friend, a lawyer, said I was a walking zombie, whatever that is, but no one seemed to notice or help me. I was going to a doctor; he couldn't.

Three months later, we were in a small apartment in Columbia. The children didn't like their schools, except Robert. He was playing ball. I was with them, but I couldn't see them grieving. I wanted to die so bad. I could not give him up.

One day, I was lying across the bed, watching Debra and another little first grader playing in front of the dresser, two little girls. I fell off to sleep. I was in a room as dark as it can be, and Fred called my name. I tried to find a light switch, but he told me not to turn the light on. I could not see him. He came over to where I was and put his arms around me, kissed me, and told me he loved me, but he could not stay but a few minutes. When I put my arms around him, I don't know what it was, but I knew in my heart I would never see him again in this world. Then he started telling me if I could open my eyes, I would know I was not alone over and over. As he left me he said, "We will take care of you."

It was like I had to bury him again in my heart and go on for the children. He loved them, and they needed me. I had four at home. Debra had just started school, one in the army, single, and three married. I felt like I was in a big world, and no one cared about me. No one really could help me. I was going to a doctor, but he could not help me.

That hole I was in was too deep, dark, and lonely, and I wanted to die so bad. I did not get anything from the plant where he was killed to help me raise the children or pay for his funeral.

Adele lived in Madison, so I came up there and bought a house. I put nearly every penny I had down on it. Now we were in a strange place, did not know anyone but Adele and her family, and I wasn't able to work. I didn't even wait for Robert to get his ball picture. He was so hurt, and I really was sorry about it later and even now.

I love my children and was taking care of them, or I was keeping them in school and provided food for them. I really didn't realize how much they missed their daddy. I was in such a shape myself.

One evening, when I cooked dinner for us, I realized I was cooking all the food I had except some cereal for their breakfast the next morning. I did not tell them, and I knew I did not have any money to buy more food. I cried and prayed nearly all night. I would say, "Lord, let someone have compassion on me and send me a check so I can buy some groceries."

The next morning, I fixed their breakfast, and they went on to school. I sat down and waited for the mail to come. He did not leave me anything. I prayed and cried some more. I did not want my kids to come home hungry and nothing to eat. I am one person who can't ask anyone to help me. God is the only one I can talk to, but I love to help others. This is when I started really believing in angels. I know they are God's helpers. While I was praying that morning, I remembered the dream I had that day in Columbia when Fred told me they would take care of me.

I got up and got a pen and paper and wrote a few things down, enough to make a few meals. Then I laid my head on my grocery bill and prayed. I said, "Lord, You said that You would take care of me and the children now. I have to have some groceries." I thought no more about not having any money. I got ready and got into my car. I couldn't even drive and went to Kroger. That is when they were in the Madison Square Shopping Center. I parked close to the store. I got out of the car to go inside. When I dropped my keys in that empty purse, a man standing there said, "Don't drop your keys in there."

I said while I was getting them out, "I always do." I looked around. There was no man standing there. I stood there holding my keys a few seconds. Then I said I just imagined I heard that, and I dropped them back in my purse. When I did that, the man said again very sternly, "Don't drop your keys in there." I got them out again. I looked around, and no one was standing there. I looked at the cars. No one was in them. I stood there a little while, shocked. Then I thought something might happen to my keys. I leaned up against the car and opened another part of my purse and dropped my key in and closed it real quick.

Then it dawned on me that it looked like money in there. I opened my purse and looked. Lying straight in the bottom of my empty purse was what looked like a handful of paper money. I did not take time to count it. I closed my purse, slammed the car door shut, and ran every step of the way to the store, got me a cart and enough groceries for a couple of weeks. Then I pushed my cart through, and they told me how much they were. I reached in my purse and got that money, paid for my groceries, and took some bills home with me. I don't remember how much my groceries cost or how much I took home with me, but I am still praising God. And that day, God reached down in that lonely hole and pulled me out.

It was a long time before I was able to go back to work, and that day when I drove to the store was the only time I could drive that car until a friend of ours changed the transmission for an automatic transmission and a son-in-law rode with me in Madison Park until I could drive well enough to get my license. The friend who changed transmissions is Judy's husband now. They have two children, a son and a daughter. When he changed them was when I was able to go to work, and since that day in 1962, I drove to the store. I have never been without groceries or enough money to buy our needs. I thank and praise God for His love and tender mercy He shows us.

After I moved to Madison, I had to be in the hospital for a few days. I had just come home, and I was in bed. I got so sick I could not get up to get myself something to help me. The kids were in the living room playing music and talking and could not hear me calling them. I just started praying, and I fell asleep. I dreamed I was in a brush arbor meeting at the edge of a big woods. I have never been in a brush arbor meeting. It had sawdust for the floor, plank seats, and a piano. Several people were there. When the preacher started to preach, I got up and walked down into the woods. I have never seen trees as tall as those trees were. I walked a long distance, and it was raining softly. I could hear the leaves crunch under my feet as I walked. I heard two voices behind me—a man's voice and a woman's voice. It did not frighten me, and I never looked back. Every once in a while, the woman would say, "Are you going to let her go?" The man's voice would say yes. I had walked a long ways when I came to a small clearing in the woods about the size of a room. In the middle of it was a big rock or a statue. The rain was running down on it. It was so clean it shone like the sun was shining on it.

I went over and got down on my knees beside it and started praying. My whole life seemed to pass before me. It was so easy to pray. I don't know how long I knelt there when the man's voice said,

"You have prayed enough. Now you can enter in." I got right up. There was a door beside me. I took hold of the doorknob. The woman's voice said, "Are you going to let her go?" There was silence; a few minutes passed. Then he called my name and said, "You can come back for a little while," and I woke up.

I was wet with perspiration. I was sobbing. My pillow was wet with tears, and I was too weak to get up. I really believe I almost died that night, and God sent me back for the children.

The next morning, Adele called me and asked me if I was sick last night. She said she prayed for me because she felt like I was sick. Could that have been the woman's voice I heard? Thank you, Jesus.

*****

When Eddie was in the eighth grade, he spent the night with his friend Ronnie. The next morning, they came to my house and went to Eddie's room. In a few minutes, they called for me to come in there. I went in to see what he wanted. They were standing in the middle of the floor, grinning real big with their caps on. At the same time, they pulled their caps off. Honestly, I almost passed out. Then I got tickled. They looked so different.

Eddie's beautiful wavy auburn hair was as white as snow, and Ronnie's beautiful black hair was the color of an orange. They had been playing with peroxide. Ronnie cut his hair off short until it grew out, but Eddie would not go outside until I went and got some hair color and put on his hair. I did not know how to use that stuff, so I got Adele to help me, and she didn't know any more than I did. I don't know who got the most of it, but he looked better when we got through even if he was standing in the bathtub. The next time, he got someone who knew how to use it until his hair grew out.

*****

When Robert got out of school, he got a job and worked a few years. Then he and a friend joined the army. After their training, they sent them both to Vietnam. He saw the war and was in it. He was injured more than once and still suffers from it. He won't talk much about it. He just says it was awful. He was fortunate to come home, and I thank the dear Lord He watched over him and those other men.

Eddie finished high school and went to college and quit college and joined the navy. He went to Florida for his training, and then he went to San Diego, California, for his training to be a radio specialist.

At that time, I was just starting to work again. Fred had bought a new Falcon to drive back and forth to work, and when he passed away, I kept it a few years, then sold it and bought myself a Chevrolet to drive to work. I had gotten it about three weeks before Eddie finished his training in California and came home.

When he got home, he had not gotten much sleep when his friends gave him a party. Coming home from the party, he fell asleep while driving the Chevrolet and ran into an electric pole. The front end on one side of his car was pushed in on Eddie's leg. They could not move the car. They just had to pull his leg out, and he was begging them to leave him in there. He was going in and out of consciousness. He was hurt real bad. A friend was with him. He wasn't hurt, just shook up real bad. He was buckled in and was asleep. Their glasses were thrown out of the car and broken.

Eddie was in the hospital for several days here, and when he was able to move, they took him to the army hospital in Clarksville. That was during the Vietnam War. When Eddie was better, they sent him to Guantanamo Bay, Cuba. That is where he was stationed.

After my car was wrecked, I had to have a car to drive to work, so I bought myself a little sports car Vega. It was a nice little car, and I loved to drive it. But in about a month, somebody stole it off the parking lot while I was working, and it was never found. I bought myself an old Falcon, as I thought no one would want it. The man told me the motor and tires were real good. Not too long afterward, it gave me the scare of my life. I was going to work one morning. I was starting across a four-lane highway. I got across the first lane when the motor died, and I could not restart it. I was so scared. There were no houses close by. I started to get out to seek help when I saw Dupont's third shift had started home. The cars were coming around that curve down that straight stretch, going fast and blowing their horns for me to move on, and I could not. I was afraid someone would get killed, and I was praying it wouldn't be me. I was too scared to move. I was saying, "Lord help me" over and over. It sounded like a big motor pulled in behind my car, and I passed out.

When I came to, I was sitting with my hands on the wheel, and I was looking out the window. I was fixing to turn down Old Hickory Boulevard. I had crossed over the median and the other two lanes of traffic, and that little motor was purring like a new one. I looked to see who was in the car with me, but there was no one. I started crying and praising God for sending me someone to drive my car across that four-lane highway. I told everybody who would listen that day about it. We serve a wonderful God. He knows where we are and what we need all the time and is so willing to help us.

Later I had taken Debbie to school one morning, and I was almost home when a lady late for work ran a stop sign and totaled my little car. The police gave her a ticket, and she bawled him out because he didn't give it to me. She told him I ran in front of her. He asked her what were stop signs for? I'm thankful it didn't hurt either of us bad. I sold that little car for fifty dollars, and the motor was still purring like a new one, and I was without a car again.

When Debbie was singing with the Singing Twenty Group at church, Judy, Debbie, and I went to visit my sister-in-law in Dallas, Texas. We stayed several days and planned to come home on Friday morning. Debbie was sick all night Thursday night, and Judy didn't get much sleep, but we still left at five thirty anyway. It was hard for Judy to drive a distance any time of day without getting sleepy. She got so sleepy that day. I kept a cold wet cloth for her to wash her face nearly all day, but anyway, I think she drove with her eyes half closed. I was so scared and nervous, and Debra slept almost all day. She was supposed to sing Saturday night, and we had to get home so she could practice. We got back to Madison at 3:30 p.m. Then she took Debra to Donelson to practice, and they had called off the singing. What a day to remember. That is the last trip I have taken like that.

After my little Falcon was totaled, I had a hard time getting to and from work every day. One Saturday night, Jimmy came to work and picked me up. He had come home and had gotten married and lived fairly close to me. When we got home that night at about ten thirty, my front door was just pushed like someone had been inside. He went in and checked every room. No one was there, so he left. I stood in the front door and watched him until he got out of the driveway. Then I closed and locked the door. We had only left one light on in the kitchen. It shone through a window into the living room. When I turned around to go into the room, it looked like a big fog had settled in the room. I could not go into it.

I had a stereo close to the door. I put on one of Jimmy Swaggart's albums to play. To me, that album *There Is a River* is anointed. When it started playing, I sat down in a chair by the door to listen to it. In a few minutes, I felt the presence of someone coming through the door. I could not see anyone, but I followed it by its presence. It went across the room and sat down on the couch in front of me. The feeling of loneliness left, and the heavenly cloud disappeared. It felt so peaceful.

When the album finished playing, it was getting late, and I had to wash and roll my hair for the next day for church. I went into the kitchen and set my hair dryer up on the table. I went in and washed my hair, dried it some, then I went into the den to roll it up. It seemed like my heavenly visitor was with me all the time. I decided I wanted to hear that album again even though it was late. I went back in the living room and put the record back on to play. After I had sat down again, in a few minutes, my angel came through the door from the den, and he blocked out all the light in that door for a second. He was so large. He was bigger than the door. I almost fell out of my chair; it frightened me so bad. He sat down again, and in a few more minutes, he was gone. I stayed up awhile to calm my nerves and enjoy the wonderful peace I felt. Thank you, Jesus.

Jimmy found me a little Oldsmobile. It was a nice little car. One day, I was working. Debra was in school, and when she came home, she decided to go and spend the night with a girlfriend. It was raining when she left home but not very bad. When she got a short ways from home a flash flood came. She was right beside Madison Park. Some men had been playing ball in the park, and when it started raining, they had gone under a shed instead of leaving. They saw Debra when the car hydroplaned and slammed into a tree. A man at Madison Towers was looking out of a window, and he saw the car and called 911. An ambulance came right out.

She was unconscious when the men got to the car. They took a ball bat and broke out a window so they could pry the door open to get to her. The steering wheel was bent back. The key was broken off. Even the mirror in her travel case was broken. The car was one more wreck.

My sister in Columbia was watching the news. It showed them putting her in the ambulance. She said they called a DOA in. She said she told the ones with her that was Debbie. They called me at work, and my manager came and told me Debbie had been in a little wreck, but she wasn't hurt. She took me to the hospital. When we got there, a policeman was waiting for me. The first thing he said to me was "Now, don't you fuss on that little girl," and I asked him "Should I?" He said they were moving my car. About that time, they came bringing her out of X-ray on a bed. I looked down at her. She was conscious, and she looked up at me and started crying, saying, "Mama, let's go home." Blood was coming out of her ears, nose, and mouth, and probably her eyes. A big cut was across one eye, and her nose was broken and lying over on her face. You can imagine how I felt, and I was helpless, and every time she would see me, she would start crying and begging me to take her home. I had to stay out of her sight as much as I could.

It took the doctor a long time to put her nose back right, but he did a good job. The next night, she told me the nicest little preacher rode to the hospital with her. She said he kept telling her, "Honey, you're going to be all right." She was probably unconscious on the way to the hospital. There sure wasn't a preacher in there with her. It was probably the Lord talking to her because she recovered so quickly. In two or three weeks, she was back in church singing again. I praise the Lord for her quick recovery and for His compassion and for His wonderful love He shows us and for letting her face, nose, and body heal so well without even a scar. Thank you, Jesus.

I think it hurt me nearly as bad as it did her. And I was without a car again. I went without a car for a while. I really needed one bad to keep from bothering other people so much. This time, I bought a little Buick, and I kept it a long time.

Judy went to college. She teaches school now. She married about a year after she finished school. They have two children. When their son was born, he was premature, and the baby had a problem. She was having a very hard time. They called me to come up there. Debra and I went to the hospital. I stayed with her until they took her into the delivery room. Her husband was working. I don't know why they waited until the baby was born before they called him. After the baby arrived, they waited a long time before we could see him. They let us see him for a few seconds, then they pulled the curtains shut. In a few minutes, they came by the door, running. They had him in a bag on a table. As they passed the door, they asked anyone who wanted to ride with him in the ambulance to come on.

His other grandmother and I went with him to the Vanderbilt Hospital. They were at the door waiting for him when we got there. In a few minutes, they had tubes and cords all over him. He was so tiny. Mrs. Nichols called the Oral Roberts prayer group, and all the families were praying for both Judy and the baby. She was in a real bad condition also. Freddy came to the hospital when they called him. He went to see Judy first, then he came on over to see the baby. He said when he got over there, two doctors met him at the door with a paper to sign so they could take his eyes and body parts if he didn't make it. They didn't think he would live until morning. But he would not sign the papers. They gave him a gown and told him to stand by his bed awhile.

Freddy went home by himself that night. He said he wanted to be alone. The next morning, when he got to the hospital, his little bed was empty. He thought he had died until he saw a nurse smiling. She told him, "We had a miracle last night. We have him in an incubator now, breathing by himself." Three or four days later, mother and baby both got to go home. Miracles still happen today. Praise the Lord.

Here is a little one on me. One morning at work, I was the only one on the floor that morning in our department. The little girl in the deli ran a real good special on sliced ham, and that was real good ham. I ran across the aisle and told her to wrap me a pound and I would pay for it when I picked it up at quitting time, and she did. We all did that.

A little later, a guard came over and asked me if I had bought any of that ham. I said yes, I bought a pound. She asked if I paid for it. I said, no, not until quitting time when I pick it up. She went to the manager and asked her if I bought some ham. She told her no, her girls would not do that, but we did sometimes, and she did too. A little later, another guard came over and asked me the same thing. I was called up front for a price check. The security guard came up to me and put his arm on my shoulder and said, "Mrs. Webb, I believe we are in trouble. I bought some of that ham also." Now I was worried. Not much longer, a lady from the office came to me and asked me the same thing. I always told them the same thing—no, I did not pay for it; I would when I quit. Then she said, "Are you sure?" That's all they would ever say. Now I was angry.

I was called to the checkout lane for a price check. I see the store manager coming. He was a tall guy. He came to me, laid his arm around my shoulder, and he leaned over and said to me real low, "Mrs. Webb, did you buy some of that ham this morning?"

I looked at him, scared, and I said, "That ham again. Yes, I bought a pound of it, but now I don't want it. You can have that old ham because I don't want it."

He started laughing, and I didn't see anything funny about it. He knew I was nervous. That is what they wanted to do, to see if I would change my answer. He said, "I don't want the ham. All I want to know is did you pay for it?"

I said, "Mr. Ezell, I have told everyone I bought a pound. I would pay for it at quitting time, but now I don't want it."

He said, "That is all I wanted to know, and I want you to get your ham and enjoy it." Like I could after all of this aggravation, but I did.

The little girl in the deli had some money by the register. They asked her when they saw it why it was lying there. She told them I had bought a pound and paid her, and she had not had time to put it in the register, which was not true, and she found out she had made a mistake saying that.

*****

The children had married one at a time until they were all gone, and I was alone again and lonely. I am proud of my daughters-in-law and my sons-in-law. I think God sent me the best. I love them all.

Debra was the last one to leave. I loved my children so much. Now they were all gone from home. She married on a Saturday. The next morning, I woke up, and the house was so quiet and lonely. I got so depressed. I should have turned over and gone back to sleep, but I didn't. I was raised in a large family, and I had a large family myself. I was used to noise, music, singing, laughter, and so forth. It was never quiet. I missed it so much and still do after all these years.

I got up and got ready and went to church. I thought I would go home with Adele. She lived close to the church where we went. Maybe I would feel better. I had not told her how bad I felt. When I got to church, I was a little late. I went in and sat down beside her. As if she knew what I was thinking, she looked at me and said, "Mama, I would ask you to go home with us today, but we are going to Roy's brother and family and spend the afternoon with them." Any other time I would have been proud of her, but today I needed someone to talk to, but she didn't know.

Well, that old devil was sitting on the seat behind me that day. He heard her. He leaned over my shoulder and said, "If she loved you, she would have taken you home with her," and I said, "Yes, she would have." That turned him loose on me. Then I was depressed and oppressed. I didn't hear much what the preacher said that day, and when the service was over, I went to my car and left. I don't know how I made it home those thirteen miles because I was crying so hard. By the time I got home that day, I felt like not any of my children loved me or anyone else. The devil kept telling me neither my children nor anyone loved me. When I got home, I went in and fixed myself a sandwich. I could not eat a bite. I soaked it in tears. Finally, I started telling the Lord these thoughts I was having, like *Why don't you just die? No one would find you for days. You're all alone, aren't you? Where are they?* I got the feeling to go in the living room and put that album I loved so well, *There Is a River*, on the stereo. When it started to play, I was still crying. I looked up and said, "Lord, I have cried this river full of tears by myself."

Judy had given me a little clock when she started teaching. It was hanging over the stereo. I looked up to see what time it was, but the clock wasn't up there. I got a glimpse of the old rugged cross hanging on my wall, and Jesus was hanging on the cross with the crown of thorns on His head. When I looked up, He was looking down, and He spoke audibly to my heart the three sweetest words I have ever heard—I love you.

I fell on my knees and asked God to forgive me. I knew my children loved me, and I had friends who cared. I asked God to never let me forget that day, and I've shed many tears thinking about it. I have never felt sorry for myself again. Lonely and a little depressed, yes, but never unloved. Yes, the devil goes to church sometimes, and he will talk to you. Don't ever give him a chance.

I was by myself so much I got to thinking maybe I needed some kind of protection. No one had ever tried to bother me, but I told Jimmy to get me a pistol. Now I am afraid of guns. I have never shot one but once. I shot at a tin can on a post and knocked it off. He bought me one and a box of shells. After he left, I threw it on top of my wardrobe. Everyone was afraid to come to see me, afraid of getting shot. I never had any company—just me and my gun.

The young friends around had a party one night and had a bunch of stuff left and wanted to give it to me, but they were afraid to knock on my door. They called me and told me it was on my back steps. It was late, and I had to go through the garage to get it. It was so nice of them. I appreciated it, but I hated going outside that late.

I had never loaded the gun one time. One night, I got it down and put a shell in every hole. I laid it on my nightstand. No one would bother me tonight. I went to bed and went to sleep. That very night, around midnight, I was sound asleep when some man hollered to the top of his lungs at the corner of my house where the bed was sitting. I jumped up in bed. He scared me to death. I could not move a joint in my body, just my neck. I was completely frozen. I would turn my head and look at that gun lying there loaded, and I was helpless.

I had never been like that in my whole life. I don't know how long I sat there like that, but I knew then I did not need a pistol. I started praying, "Lord, build a hedge around me so high that man can't climb over where I am," and I lay back down and went back to sleep. The next morning, I shook the shells out and threw it back on top of the wardrobe until I sold it. I did not need it anymore. God had always protected us.

That winter was a terrible winter—so much ice and snow. Wayne was a plumber, and the weather was so bad. There wasn't much building going on, and he carried me back and forth to work. I couldn't drive in it. He didn't get much work back then, so he helped me. Wayne and his son, Jeffrey, moved in with me for a while. Jeff was nine years old. He went to work with me a lot of times when school would be closed from the weather. He helped our stock boy a lot. One day, he was sitting on the bottom of my work cart, and we were laughing and talking while I worked. The customers could not see him from the other side of the rack, and they thought I was talking to myself. They would look at me so funny. Some of them would go to the end and look and see him and start laughing. That would tickle Jeff. He went to the shoe department one day and brought a pair of shoes back big enough for his daddy and said, "Mom, I sure do need these shoes." I told him if he needed them to go back and get a pair that fit him. So he did, and when he came back with them, he said, "Mom, I have the money to pay for them." I knew he didn't carry that much money around in his pocket, but I said, "Okay."

When quitting time came, and we were checking out, he had his little shoes in his hand in front of me. When it came his turn to check out, he set them up on the counter and looked up at me and said, "Mom, I don't have any money."

I said, "Well, I have." I couldn't keep from laughing, and I'm glad I did, or we both would have been backing out. He always liked to pull tricks on me. Kids are so sweet.

When I had surgery and had to stay in bed for a week without getting up unless it was necessary, Jeff was in play school, and his mama was working. He wouldn't go to school. He wanted to stay with me, and he did that for a whole week. She would fix him lunch and bring him over to my house. He would divide his lunch with me and get us some water every day. He would bring his case full of little hot wheels, and we would take pillows and make mountains and valleys and have races. I'll bet you can't guess who always won? He was good. He would stay on the bed with me all day, and we would play.

He had a basketball water game, and he was good at that too. We had lots of fun. It would have been awfully lonely without him. He is married now and has two sons and a daughter, and he races with real race cars now. He is good.

When his little sister, Tonya, was around that age, I kept her sometimes also. I had a little rocker that would pop when you rocked in it. She called it my "pop pop" chair. Her Granddaddy Legg would sing a little song to her, something about a cow. All she remembered was "The ole cow ate the little girl's hand off." Every time she got tired or sleepy, she would get my hand and say, "Mom, rock in the pop pop chair," and while I was rocking her, she wanted me to sing that little song to her. I didn't know it or even the tune, so I put a tune to it, and I would rock her a long time, sometimes singing "the ole cow ate the little girl's hand off." Sometimes I wanted to kill that ole cow, but I just kept on rocking. She was a sweet little girl and still is.

I didn't get the pleasure to keep all my grandchildren. Some of them lived too far away. Gwen lived in Florida for years while her children grew up.

I lived close to Adele a few years when I first moved to Madison. I rode to church with them a lot before Donna was old enough to start school. She was so quiet. She kept her finger in her mouth a lot. Her daddy even promised to buy her a pony if she would quit, but she wouldn't. One night, I noticed her coming home from church. I noticed her sitting so quiet. I said, "Donna, if you quit keeping your finger in your mouth, I will go to town and buy you the prettiest thing I could find.

A few days after that, Adele and I were in town. She said, "What are you going to get Donna? She has quit."

I said, "Really?" Man, I didn't know where to look. We looked at everything in Madison that day. I couldn't find what I wanted, but I bought her a large doll buggy, almost big enough for a baby. She liked it all right I think. She had a big doll. That was the best thing I could find.

When I would leave their house, I would give Donna a little change. Wanda and Debbie were in school. One day, Steve followed us to the door. He was about eighteen months old I guess. When I gave Donna some change, he whirled around and went through the room screaming. I thought he was sick. I said, "Adele, what is wrong?"

"You didn't give him any money," she said.

"Adele, I thought he was too young to even notice," I said. I went to him, and it took nearly all I had to quiet him. You can believe after that if I give to one, I give to all.

Debra and Wanda played together a lot. One day, they were playing in the yard. Roy had set out some young trees, and he told Wanda one of them was hers. That day they were playing, and they must have stripped all the leaves off and maybe a limb. I don't know. When Roy came home from work, he got on to them about it, and Wanda told him it was her tree. He spanked both of them. I guess she gave the tree back to him. They were real young.

Steve could run fast when he was young. When he was around two years old, Adele and I were in JCPenney, shopping for material. We both sewed a lot then. I had just picked up a bolt of cloth in my arms, and I looked around. I saw Steve as he went out the front door running. I never took the time to lay the bolt down. I ran through that store as fast as I could run, and up the sidewalk I went. I finally caught him, and I caught a lot of attention also. I guess the people thought I was trying to get away with that cloth. Thank God he stayed on the sidewalk.

When I got back to the store, the manager was standing in the door laughing. He knew what I was doing. He said he (Steve) liked to have gotten away this time. He thought it was funny. I said yes, he did. I guess I looked funny running with a bolt of cloth in my arms.

I wish I could have spent more time with all my grandchildren, great-grandchildren, and my great-great-grandchildren. I do the best I can, but I love all of them. I was blessed to live to see all of my children grow up and marry and see their family grow up and see a lot of my great- and great-great-grandchildren after being told by three doctors in Tennessee, Missouri, and California I would not live to see my children grow up. I thank you, dear God, for my many blessings.

Now I will tell what happened the last Christmas I was working. Someone brought in a big cake to the layaway. All the employees were going in there, eating a little of that cake and coming back for more, and they were all so happy. Man, they all had the Christmas spirit. I was about the only one who was working in my department. I thought, *I want a piece of that cake if it makes you feel that good.* I was tired. I went to the window and told them I wanted a piece of cake. I heard someone say, "Gracie, just give her a bite off of the first layer." I did not understand that, but I took it and ate it. It tasted pretty good. In a little while, I was called to the service desk for a price check. I went to take it. When I got up there, I could not stand up. I was holding to the customer. We were both concerned. I thought I was fixing to pass out. I knew I was tired.

The little girl behind the desk called the back and asked them if I had been eating that cake. They told her I had a bite, so she got me a glass of ice, and I ate some ice and made it back to the layaway. Then they sent me to eat my lunch, and I was okay. Two weeks later, they started teasing me, and they told me that was a Rum Cake with a lot of rum in it. I sure am glad they only gave me a bite of it.

These last few years, I've been around my children more and spend more time now with my children. I visit them a lot. I see Debra more than the others. She lives close to me. She is always coming over and doing things for me.

I had to work all the time after Fred passed away, and that is why I had to stay at home so much.

When Brandon, Robert' s little boy, was six years old and Clay, Debra' s little boy, was five years old, they had been out playing ball one day. They were outside, and Debra was inside listening to them through a window. One of them said, "You sure did play well today." The other one said, "You did better than I did." "No, you did the best…" On and on they went talking. She said it sounded so sweet. Even now that they are grown and Clay is married, they are still so kind and precious. I think all my grandchildren are. I love them all.

I will never forget when my children were real young, when they would be outside playing. All of them would bring me little bouquets. I kept them sitting around. They would be playing in the yard and see a pretty weed or something blooming, break it off or pull it up, and bring it to me. Sometimes they would be so wilted, but they wanted me to have them. They would hold their little arms straight out and say, "I love you this much." They were so sweet.

Jewell's little boy, Jerry, would always bring me flowers like that also, and I love him too.

Judy teaches school, mostly the second or third grade, or that is her choice. She told me one day she was kind of moving slow, and she did not have time to fix her hair (this is before she married) before she left home for school. So she put on a wig, thinking no one would notice. She said she kept noticing this little girl looking at her. Then she got up and came up to her and said, "Miss Webb, I didn't know today was Halloween." She wanted to get dressed up also. She was so embarrassed. She said she had never worn that wig again. Children can say the sweetest things. Just ask Judy. She still teaches school. She and her husband and family live near the mountains in East Tennessee.

I spend nearly every Christmas with them. The mountains are always beautiful. Each season has its own beauty, except when it snows. I like to be at home then. There is no place like home when it snows.

In May 1997, I went back to our old homeplace just to see how things looked now. It was so lonely. There was a little storehouse by the road almost in front of our house, but our house was farther up on the hill. They had torn them both down. The pretty trees that were in the yard and the shrubbery were gone. The pretty crepe myrtle that was by the porch and the beautiful pink rosebush by the road were gone.

I imagined I saw Fred pick me a rose and bring it to me like he did when they were blooming.

Our new barn was old and falling apart in places. The dairy barn where we spent so much time was old and the end torn out. I looked inside. Just a cabinet on the wall was all that was left, and the doors were just hanging on. The windows were broken out. I looked where our big milk cooler sat. It wasn't there anymore. The room was full of junk.

I looked in the room where we milked so long so many times. I could see the pretty Holstein cows lined up, eating, and the big Guernsey cow we couldn't get the milkers on, Eddie almost under her, milking her by hand. He was only a child. She was so protective of him when the cow next to her would prance around. It really broke my heart.

I went up on the hill above the dairy barn and stood awhile and looked. My mind went back in time for a while. I could see Fred walking across the pasture, reaching down to pick up a rock to throw. I could hear the children laughing and playing and running with our little black-and-white dog we all loved.

I could see us driving the cows up to milk and then suppertime when we would all be around the table laughing, talking, and eating. It was so lonely.

I asked about our neighbors. They had all died or moved away. The farm had been divided into three tracts. It did not look the same.

The store where we bought our groceries is a big service station now.

But time goes on. I have no desire to ever go back. It had been thirty-five years since I moved away.

There are too many memories and too many tears. But God has always been there for me and with us...and has helped me find happiness again. Praise His holy name.

Another chapter of my life...

We were living on a large farm, running a dairy in 1961. There was an accident where my husband was working, and he was injured real bad. He had a broken leg, internal injuries, and cuts and bruises.

Three weeks later, he died in the hospital. He never came home. He was just forty-five years old. He was buried January 2, 1962, in the Garden of Memories in the Lawrenceburg Memorial Cemetery.

I was left alone with four children at home, the youngest just starting school, and a seventeen-year-old son in the army. The oldest three were married.

There was no way I could keep the farm and run the dairy without him, so I sold it and moved to Columbia to be near some of my family. I was so unhappy, and the children were too. I went into depression, which lasted a long time, but God was with us all the time.

Then we moved to Madison, Tennessee, and I bought us a nice little house. I liked it, but the children didn't. But they pretended for my sake. I lived there eighteen years, but I never ceased to be lonely.

It was about eight years before I was physically able to go to work, but I always took care of the children and kept them in school.

We went through a lot during those years. Robert was in a wreck, but he wasn't hurt bad. Then Eddie was in a wreck. The mercy of God was all that saved him. Then Debbie was going to spend the night with her girlfriend. It was raining when she left home but not very bad. A little distance from home, a flash flood came, and her car hydroplaned and slammed into a tree. It was a miracle she was still alive. The car was a total wreck. Thank God He took care of her.

Then came the Vietnam War. Robert joined the army, and they sent him to Vietnam. He saw the action and was in it. He was injured a couple of times and is still suffering from them. He won't talk about it. Then Eddie quit college and joined the navy. He was stationed in Guantanamo Bay, Cuba. He was a radio specialist. Thank the Lord they came back alive. A lot of prayers went up for those young men over there.

I have three grandsons: Jimmy, Rayford, and J. W. Cotton, all brothers (Gwen's sons) who served in the Vietnam War. J. W. was in the marines. The other two were in the fighting zone like Robert was. I praise God they all came home.

I was working every day then, and one by one, they all married and left me, and I was alone again. Their friends were my friends, and when they left home, I didn't see much of them anymore.

I lived close to one of my daughters and her family. She took me places. I loved her little children. They were so sweet, but very soon, they bought another place and moved away, and it was very lonely again.

When Robert came home from Vietnam, he went to work at the post office. Sometimes he delivered the mail to Chippington Towers. That was a retirement complex for older people.

There were a lot of older people who lived there, and they all seemed so happy to see him. Because there were several of them, he did not feel like they were lonely like I was. He started begging me to move over there. I did not want to leave my home and move. I loved my home, but to please my children, I called and checked on it. They told me I would be on a three-year waiting list, so I thought I had nothing to worry about.

So Robert took me over there on a Monday to sign up, and Thursday they called me and said I had an apartment. It nearly killed me, but everyone I talked to advised me to move, even my pastor. So I moved.

I was still working every day, but after I moved…talk about loneliness. I found it over there. It was the loneliest place in the world to me. I cried myself to sleep every night. It was so different.

I had been used to noise, music, and laughter. But there, every-thing was so quiet. If someone came in and you laughed and talked or turned your TV a little loud, your neighbor would complain. My sister-in-law from California came to visit me for one night. We laughed and talked about old times. The next morning, there was a complaint. I guess the walls were too thin or something. I don't know.

One day, I came home from work. When I came in the door, a little lady came to me and put her arms around me and said, "I'm so glad you are home. You are like a ray of sunshine."

When I went to my apartment, I broke down and cried. I know how she felt, and I was older than she was. They had dinners and parties over there. I guess I just didn't fit in.

So shortly, I wrote the Lord a letter and put it in my Bible. I told Him I knew there had to be some good Christian man out there somewhere that was as lonely as I was, and I asked Him to please send him to me. Now, I did not ask for a friend. I wanted a husband so I would have a home and someone to love and someone to love me. I guess living around so many people made me nervous.

One night, not long after that, when I came home, my phone was ringing. I worked until ten o'clock every night. I picked the receiver up and said hello. This strange voice said hello. I started laughing and said, "Mrs. Sivley, is that you?" She worked with me and was always kidding me.

I recognized a man's voice that said "No, this is Perry." It embarrassed me so bad I laid the receiver down. I was laughing hard. In a few seconds, I picked it up, and the line was still open, and I said "hello" real low. Then he said "hello" real low too. Then I apologized to him for laughing. He said he thought that was the first time anyone was that glad to hear from him.

We had never met, and this was our first conversation and was almost our last. We talked about an hour that night. I enjoyed talking to him. He was easy to talk to. It was his wife's best friend who had given him my number. She went to the church I attended and was my friend also, but I sure didn't know she had given him my telephone number.

He had a lady friend and was fixing to get married. I could not understand why he called me, but later he told me. After I laughed so hard, he just had to meet this lady once anyway just to see what I was like. But he kept calling me. He would be coming home when I would get home from work, and we would talk awhile.

He was a contractor, and he did a lot of work on our church, but I never met him. I had been a widow for eighteen years. He asked me if he could come over and take me to Sunday school at my church. I told him yes, but then I prayed he would not come.

So on Sunday, just before time for me to leave for church, he called me. He said he could not come. He had to go to a family dinner, which was not exactly true. He just wanted to see what I looked like before he met me. I know; I was feeling the same way.

I went on to church. I spent the day with my daughter and family. She lived close to the church. That evening, just before church started, he came over. He got his friend to show me to him, then he wanted to meet me. He told me later the first thought he had was *that will be my next wife.*

She took him down to the Sunday School Department and came up and got me. She said she had something to tell me. She should have said "show me."

It was kind of dark down there, and when we got down the steps, I saw this man. She just said, "Wesley this is Mrs. Webb. Minnie Belle, this is Perry." Then she walked back upstairs. We just looked at each other and never said a word. Imagine my feelings, the first man I had been close to in eighteen years like that.

I said, "Let's go up and get us a seat." It was time for the service to start. We got a seat in front of his friend, and he turned around and started talking to her. I can truthfully say I didn't like him. Then everyone was seated, and everyone was quiet.

My little granddaughter played the piano, and her husband played the drums. He looked over and saw me sitting with JW, and he hit Wanda on her knee and said, "Wanda, Wanda, Grandma's got a boyfriend."

Nearly everyone turned around and looked at us smiling. They knew him, but I didn't. I wanted to crawl under the seat, but he straightened up and smiled real big, like "uh-huh, look what I have done."

When the service was over, he turned around and started talking to his friend again. I got up and slipped past him and went up front and got my purse. I got in the middle aisle where the people were leaving. I was going home. I got outside on the first step, and someone caught hold of my arm. Some of the people in the church were watching me. His lady friend said, "Mr. Perry, take Mrs. Webb to Shoney's and get acquainted." I was not rude; I went with him.

He was hungry. He had not eaten, so he bought his dinner. I got fries and coffee. He was easy to talk to by himself, and I liked him all right. He was very friendly.

When we got back to church, every car was gone except mine. It was awfully cold. He told me to start my car and let it warm up and get back in the truck with him, and I did.

It was a couple of weeks before I saw him again, but he still called me every night. He was seeing his other friend regularly, but I did not mind at all.

I told him one night I was going to see the *Coal Miner's Daughter*. He said I did not need to go. I wouldn't like it at all. I asked him how he knew I wouldn't like it. They had been to see it that night, and he was trying to get around it without telling me. I thought it was funny since we were only friends. I really don't care for movies anyway or some of them.

Then he asked me to go to his church with him. I told him I would go again. However, I changed my mind and didn't want to go, and I told him not to come over. I didn't want to go, but he came anyway.

I went with him, but before we got to the church, I was so nervous I got sick. I tried to tell him to take me back home, but he wouldn't. He took me to his house. He lived close to the church. He drove to the back of the house and took me in his office.

It was nice and warm in there. There was a big snow on the ground outside. He went into the kitchen and came back with a bottle of Pepto-Bismol and a spoon. I took a spoonful to please him. Then he leaned over and kissed me on my forehead. He said it would make me feel better. It did, but I don't know if it was the Pepto-Bismol or the kiss. I think it was the kiss. Then we went on to church.

His wife's sisters all attended that church. They were all so nice to me. I loved all of them. A few days later, he took me to meet his sister, Alma. She was a precious lady and so much fun to be with. Then I met his son and daughter-in-law. They had two sons. The youngest one was twelve. I liked all his family. They were nice people.

I was visiting my daughter one weekend. She lived kind of close to him. He cooked me a steak dinner. He must have been awfully nervous because he was an excellent cook. He came over after me and left the steaks on the stove cooking on low and forgot to turn the stove off when he left.

The steaks were pretty well-done, but we had fun eating them. I had rather have a baked potato, but the thought is what counts, and it was sweet of him.

We had known each other a few months when he wanted to go to Debra's house to meet her, my youngest daughter. We were on our way to her house when he said, "You make me so nervous." I hadn't done or said anything to him to make him nervous, so I got a little angry, and I told him he could take me home. He didn't want to, but he did.

When we got to my house, he told me he was sick, but he left. He called me that night, and he said again he was sick. But while we were talking, he said he went to church. I told him I thought he was sick. I think he wanted to see his other friend to see which one he liked better.

I must have won. He asked me to marry him that night, but I told him to wait awhile to make sure I didn't make him nervous. He did. In a month, he asked me again, and we went and got our license and talked to my pastor about it and set a date three weeks later.

I had a lot on my mind and a lot of other things like quitting work and moving. I wanted to move to my house; he wouldn't. His office was in his house, and he still worked a lot.

So in a week, I told my pastor I wasn't getting married. He said he would pray about it, but I completely forgot to tell JW or the caterer. The day of the wedding was on a Saturday. I was over at Debbie's. He called me. When I went to talk to him, I asked him what he was doing. He said, "I'm getting ready to go to the church. I'm getting married today. What are you doing?"

"I've got to get off this phone right now," I said. I knew I had a preacher to call. When I hung up, I called my pastor. I said, "Will you marry me today?"

He started laughing and said, "Yes, come on over. I knew you'd be here. I was waiting for your call."

I didn't get to wear the dress I bought. I had left it at home, but we had a nice wedding and reception. I never told him about that because he would have laughed at me and teased me about it.

When we got to the church, JW and his son and daughter-in-law and grandson were there taking pictures. On our way home that night, we stopped at Shoney's again and ate dinner. No, we did not have a honeymoon.

When he went to pay for our meals, his money was gone. He was feeling in every pocket. I could not keep from laughing, and I felt sorry for him. He was so embarrassed. Then he went back to our table looking for it.

Two young couples had come in behind us and were sitting close to us. They were all laughing at him. They saw how worried he was, and one of them pointed to it. They saw it fall out of his pocket. They were very nice not to have gotten it and kept it. There were several dollars there. He changed his way of carrying his money after that.

My son lived in my house for a short time, and then I sold it.

That night when bedtime came, he took me and showed me the bedrooms. There was a large bedroom with twin beds. Across the hall was a smaller one with a double bed. I asked him which one was his room, and he said the small one with the double bed. He was very generous giving me my choice. I told him right quick I thought the small one with the double bed was big enough for both of us. I was not about to sleep in that big one by myself.

A few nights after that, we were watching a movie on television. He got sleepy and went to bed. I wanted to see the ending, so I stayed up until it was over.

He was asleep when I started to bed. I didn't want to disturb him, so I went into the other room and went to bed in one of the twin beds and went to sleep.

After a while, I heard a noise. It woke me. I got up looking, but he didn't see me. It was him. He was pushing the other bed across the floor beside the bed I was in. When he got it as close as he could, he lay down and went to sleep. The next morning, when we woke up, both of us were in the middle of those beds, on the hard railings.

I jumped up and said, "I thought you wanted to sleep by yourself." He just laughed. That morning we pushed the mattresses together and fixed us a nice big bed.

When we went to bed that night, it was nice. The next morning, we were in the middle again with just a sheet under us. He got up and said, "I've been thinking that double bed is big enough for both of us."

I knew it all the time. Then I asked him, "Do you really think so?" After that, he shared his bed with me peacefully.

We had a lot of fun learning each other's ways—things that we were used to doing.

He nearly always got into bed before I did. I used Mary Kay night cream, which was a little heavy and sticky. I put on a little extra. I thought he was asleep, but he wasn't. When I got in the bed, I leaned over and gave him a good night kiss, and he almost jumped out of the bed. He said, "Get up and wash your face."

I got up and said, "Okay, okay." Then I fell back across him so he couldn't move his arms and rubbed all that cream onto his face. All he could do was laugh. I was holding him.

He said, "You are the awfullest woman I have ever seen," but he liked it.

He tried to stay awake every night until I got into bed, but he couldn't always. He pulled a lot of things on me also.

One night, we were just sitting, talking, and I asked him why he called me if he had already found someone else he wanted to marry, and he told me. His wife's best friend called him one night and told him she had a friend she wanted him to meet, and she wanted to give him my phone number. He said he told her he did not want it; he had already met someone. He said he talked pretty plain to her, and she hung up. He said when he hung the receiver up, it was like there was someone else in the room with him. It was so plain, like it said, "You talked too fast to her. You do want that number. Call her back."

He said he sat there awhile, thinking about it. Then he called her. She was in bed asleep, but she gave him my number. He didn't say how long he waited before he called me, but he said that when he called me and I laughed so hard, he wanted to meet me to see why I laughed so much. I told him I learned to laugh instead of cry so much. It made me feel better.

Not too long after we married, Wayne, Anne, and boys took us to Atlanta, Georgia. We went to Stone Mountain and Six Flags Over Georgia. We enjoyed the shows while they took in the rides. We sure enjoyed that. I told JW that was our honeymoon.

Then we went on to Pineville, Georgia, to the Callaway Gardens. That was a lovely place—a beautiful place for a vacation. They said the ones who started it wanted it to be like the Garden of Eden. Well, it was beautiful—acres of all kinds of vegetables and herbs and flowers, a lot I had never seen. There was a rose garden and pretty roses and azalea blooming, flowers and shrubs everywhere. Most of the roads were named after a flower.

You could ride horses. We rode in a boat, and we walked in the paths in the woods. They had a few rides. I saw people swimming.

The little church in the woods was at the end of a trail with a picturesque little bridge—a nice place for a wedding. The organ played sometimes. It sounded so pretty through the trees. We went into the church and sat down for a little while.

Wayne rented a cabin in the woods. It was almost like being at home. They grilled hamburgers, and I believe the squirrels would have sat down and ate with us if we had invited them. They were so friendly.

That was a nice trip, and we sure enjoyed it. We went fishing a lot. We both enjoyed that. I was nearly always afraid to get out in a boat over deep water, but JW got me a jacket to wear, and I liked to go with him. We would take our lunch and stay all day. We would get off the boat to eat, and I believe the snakes knew when we were eating. It seemed like they would come to the bank thinking we would share with them. We ran from them a lot. Sometimes we would just get back in the boat to finish eating. He didn't like them any better than I did.

One day, a big goose (I guess it was; it looked like one to me. JW laughed at me.) got out of the water and came to us and tried to get our lunch, really. We went to the boat again. Later that day, on the other side of the lake, it swam to us, and we fed it a roll of crackers. It would come and take it out of my hand, but it wouldn't take one from JW. If he threw it in the water, it would eat all of it. I wish I had taken some pictures, but we never did. We sure had a lot of fun out there on the lake.

He was fishing one day real early, and he said he had caught a big one. He could hardly pull it out of the water and when he did, it was a big snake. It wouldn't let go of the bait. He had to reel it in and knock it off with a paddle. I was afraid it would come into the boat, but it didn't.

We went to Kentucky Lake a few times. He caught a lot of fish. We ate them and froze them. He sure could cook a good fish dinner. He was a good cook.

He took up jug fishing a lot. He would spread them around. One day, he saw this fish get on the jug; I didn't. It pulled the jug under the tree limb to the bank. I always had to pick the jugs up. When we left this day, he backed the boat up under the limbs and told me to get it. When I picked it up, it was a big fish, and it tried awfully hard to stay in the water. I almost fell in, trying to hold on to the jug.

He started laughing. He told me to ease it around to the side of the boat. Then he told me to pull it up in the boat. I did that too, and I almost fell out, trying to get away from it and getting wet. That was the most I ever saw him laugh. I knew it was funny but not for me. He finally took care of it. He just wanted to have some fun, and he did, more than he bargained for.

My son Wayne and his wife took us to Pigeon Forge a couple of times. We sure did enjoy riding in that boat in the cave. I don't believe they have that ride now.

After we were married a few months, he and his son built a big family room at the back of our house so we could have some family get-togethers. He only had one son, and I had four sons and four daughters and all of them were married with children.

Our first Christmas, we got a real big tree. We put it in one corner. His youngest grandson decorated it mostly by himself It was beautiful. All of our family was there, and we all had a wonderful time.

We had quite a few get-togethers before JW passed away. All of us miss those big dinners we had in those days.

That first Christmas, Valerie was about one year old and Leah was around two years old. JW always called her Lil. When she was three, she was really talking well. She would tell him, "My name is not Lil, it is Leah." They would argue awhile, and then he would say, "All right, Leah." When she would turn around, he would say Lil. She would just stomp her foot and go on. He always called her that, and she got to the point where when she came in she would go to him and say, "Granddaddy, Lil is here." He would always laugh. She and Valerie loved Granddaddy Perry, and he loved them dearly.

We had just been married a few weeks when he had to go to the doctor—a lung specialist he went to regularly. Whooping cough settled in his lungs when he was six years old. It left him with problems.

I heard the doctor tell him that day his lungs were almost thin like paper and looked like a honeycomb. He was in the hospital a lot. He just wouldn't give up. He had to take so much medicine. You had to know him, or you wouldn't think anything was wrong with him. I didn't until we were married.

He worked for about a year after we married, then he had a bad heart attack. It almost killed him, but he got all right. Then in a few months, he had to have open-heart surgery. He couldn't fish much after that, and he loved that so much. His son and friends would take him sometimes.

He kept making a big garden. He would help me can and freeze a lot of stuff, and we had a lot of company. He enjoyed that.

I had two daughters living in Okeechobee, Florida. We started going there every winter and staying a while. The first time we went, we stayed two weeks and came home. Our house was so cold and a big snow was on the ground. We got us another plane ticket and went back and stayed the rest of the winter.

I liked Florida. The last time we went, we visited the alligator farm. We took a lot of pictures. When we were leaving, we were in the walkway over the water, and a man and woman with a little girl were coming in the water, and they were so calm. The little girl had some bread they had given to her to feed the alligators. She dropped a slice in that water and five or six heads suddenly grabbed at it. I sure would hate to have fallen in that water. I'm sure you wouldn't have gotten out alive.

JW liked to fish in the Okeechobee Lake. It was a good place to fish. We all had some good fish fries when we were there. Once, my son-in-law and JW were fishing somewhere around their home, and he caught a mudfish. Tuck kept telling him to cut it loose; it would bite him, but he wouldn't, and it bit him real hard. When he got it loose, he was so mad at it he stomped it in the ground and came home. Tuck still laughs about that. I would like to have seen that.

We had been to Fort Myers once. It was kind of late when we started home. A little way out, we stopped and ate dinner. JW saw some chocolate doughnuts, and he went and got us one apiece. The others were still eating dinner.

Valerie, my little granddaughter, was six or seven years old. She saw him, and she came over and asked me for half of mine. I gave it to her. I can't imagine what that chocolate did to me.

We had just gotten back in the van when I started talking, and I couldn't stop. I was so hyper I could hardly sit in that van. My two sons-in-law were sitting in the front two seats, JW and Craig, my grandson, in the middle seat, and I was between Gwen and Judy in the back seat, and Valerie was in her mom's lap.

Well, I would hear them in front say, "Is she never going to hush?" I kept on. JW wanted to go to sleep. He would look back at me and say, "Minnie, aren't you sleepy?" I would say "not yet." Gwen would talk and grunt until her eyes would shut. Then Judy would do the same thing. That didn't bother me a bit. I kept right on talking. Finally, Valerie woke up. She and I talked and sang and played games until we got to their house in Okeechobee. Then I got out and went right to bed. It was terrible. I had never been like that before.

I said then I would never get mad again at a hyper person. If it is like I was, they can't help what they do. I know they wanted to put me out and let me walk home but hated to. That was one more special trip for me. Since then, JW saw to it that I would not eat another chocolate doughnut.

Both my daughters have moved back here now. One moved to Columbia, Tennessee (Gwen and Tuck), and Judy and Freddy moved to Dayton.

Once, we had company coming for dinner, and I had a big pot of fresh green beans cooking. JW came through the kitchen and checked them, and he thought I did not have them seasoned enough, so he helped me. I did not see him, and I didn't know it.

But I will say every bean was eaten, and they were the best beans I had ever eaten. When the company left, I asked him if he didn't help me some with those beans. He said, "A little bit." I asked him how much a little bit is, and he told me. He started to pour a little bacon dripping in them and spilled the whole jar in them. He said he tried to dip some of it out but couldn't get much. I'll bet we all got a thousand fat grams while enjoying every one of them.

He was an outdoorsman. He said he hunted a lot when he was younger. We drove to the lake a lot just to see the scenery. We saw pretty birds and ducks and small turtles on the limbs out in the water and beautiful trees.

Wayne and Jeff took us to Chattanooga once to the Aquarium. We saw a lot of fish in their natural habitat. One big fish was on a ledge. We watched it a long time hoping it would move, but it never did. We enjoyed that trip also.

We rode around a lot. I guess we just explored. We got lost so many times. It wasn't much fun unless we did. We'd drive out in the woods, trying to find a place where he had fished or hunted. I'd tell him we were lost, and he would say "not yet." When he would find his way out, he would say, "I told you, just keep turning right and you will get out."

Once, we were lost in the woods like that, and when we found our way out, I was hungry, and we saw a little church, kind of, on a hill. They were having some kind of dinner. I begged him to stop and eat with them. I told him they wouldn't care, but he would not do it. We got lost a lot, but we had fun.

One Sunday, after church service was over, JW wanted to go to Portland to see one of his friends. I don't know how we missed our turn, unless we started out wrong. We had been there before. We drove for miles and miles. I told him we should have already been there a long time ago. He would say keep looking for the sign, and I did.

A little later, I saw a billboard that said something about Chicago on it. I started patting my hair and smoothing out my dress, and then I said, "I'm so glad I'm all dressed up. I have always wanted to go to Chicago."

He said real quick (he knew I always talked to the billboards when he didn't talk), "Where did you see that?"

I said, "On a billboard back there. You were driving so fast I couldn't read it."

The first place he could find to stop, he stopped, and he asked the attendant how far it was to Portland. The man did not know of any place around like that. He called another man over and asked him if he knew. That man didn't know either. He told JW, "I believe you have passed it or something." So we turned around and started back home the way we had come.

We rode for hours, several hours. We did not get to go to church that night, nor did we see a sign saying Portland, nor did we find Portland, but we sure had a wonderful time trying.

We would get up early a lot of mornings and get in the car and just drive. Sometimes we would go down in Alabama where he was raised. We would nearly always find an old friend or a distant relative of his he had not seen for years. He enjoyed that, and I did too. It was interesting.

Sometimes we would take his sister Alma with us. She was always fun to be with. One day, Alma and I were talking about when we were kids and growing up and when we got married and learning to cook and do housework and things like that. She said she didn't know much about cooking either. She worked like I did.

Both of our husbands loved chocolate pies, and neither one of us knew how to bake one. She told me when they first married, they lived at the edge of the woods, in a trailer, and the trailer was kind of high off the ground. He hunted a lot, and he had a big hound dog to hunt with. He kept his dog tied close to the house, and it stayed under the house a lot.

She said she started making a chocolate pie every day, trying to learn how, and it wouldn't taste good, and she threw it up under the house for the dog to eat so he wouldn't know about it until she learned.

She said one day, he came home early, and he took the dog and went to hunt, but he wasn't gone very long until he came back. She said he came in and sat down, then he said to her so seriously, "I don't know what in the world has got into that old hound dog. He's got so fat he won't chase anything. He can't run as fast as I can."

She said she jumped up and went into another room to laugh. She knew what was wrong with his old dog. He had been eating too many pies, but she sure didn't tell him. We laughed so much together.

My experience was a little different. I didn't know how to cook anything when I married. I worked all the time when I was young on the farm, and when I was older, I went to work in a factory, but I soon learned how to cook. I could fry a delicious fried fruit pie, but chocolate pie…no. He wanted one so bad. One day, I thought I would surprise him, and I did, man.

I baked one. It looked so pretty. I was so proud of myself. When he came home, I said, "Honey, I baked you a chocolate pie today." He could hardly wait to get a piece of it.

That night while we were eating dinner, our neighbors came in the kitchen to talk awhile. He ate hurriedly to get a piece of pie, and when he started to cut himself a piece, honestly, we didn't have a knife in the kitchen sharp enough to cut that crust.

Bob, the neighbor man, saw him trying so hard. He said Fred, "Do you want me to go home and get my saw and help you?" Like I wasn't embarrassed enough.

He said, "No, I can make it." He knew I had tried.

I wanted to throw the pie in Bob's face, but the filling was edible. It tasted pretty good.

I didn't try again for a few years, and I couldn't find a recipe he liked. One day, I sat down and wrote one myself. We all loved it, and we still use it when we bake one. It is in our church cookbook.

Alma and I were more like sisters. I loved her. She died in a few years of cancer. We sure did miss her.

When JW had to have cataract surgery on his eyes and couldn't see well to drive anymore, that was really the beginning of his troubles. He liked to drive, not ride with someone, and we didn't go to many places after that. I had driven for years until I married him. Then he did the driving. I could drive to church or the grocery store but nowhere else.

We went to visit Vina, his sister in Alabama, and stayed a couple of nights with her, and her husband and his son Wayne came after us. He brought us home through the Natchez Trace. We had never been that way before. It was real nice.

We stopped at a roadside market coming home. JW bought some fresh corn. When we got home, he stayed outside awhile and shucked it so I could work it up. When he came in the house, he came up to me and asked me where the bathroom was. He kind of whispered like someone else was there. He said, "If you would show me where it is, I will go and wash up." I took him and showed him where it was, and then he said thank you like I was a stranger. That really bothered me because he had the house built and had lived there for many years.

I never told anyone about it, but I noticed he started changing. If I did not feel like going to church, he would get angry with me and ask me who kept me in church before I met him. I told him I kept myself in church because I liked to go to church.

He wanted to go especially at night. I had to do all the driving, sick or well, and sometimes I could not go. I could never see too well to drive at night, but he could not understand. The doctor said he was having ministrokes of the brain. His mind kept getting more and more mixed up. He was pretty good in the daytime but lots worse at night. He could not sleep but a little nap and then up again. Some nights, I would cook breakfast as much as three times. He would sit down and eat a few bites. I guess that is what kept us both going.

One day, I went in the den to see about him. He was sitting in the middle of the den floor, warming his hands over a big fire. The blaze was going around him.

He had filled a pasteboard box full of newspapers and set them on fire. I grabbed the box up and sat it on the heater and ran and got a wet towel and took it outside to burn. He looked up at me and smiled and said, "Why did you do that? I had built us a fire."

He always kept a good fire in the heater when it was cold outside, and he thought that was what he was doing.

He always helped me cook when he was well. He was a wonderful cook, and when he got sick and sometimes came through the kitchen and saw something cooking that looked done to him, he would pick the pan up and start pouring it on the stove, thinking he was pouring it in a bowl. If I said anything to him about it, it hurt him. He'd say, "I was trying to help you." It was heartbreaking. That went on for several long months.

He fell so many times, and I had to pick him up by myself. I know God sent me an angel sometimes to help me, especially when I was sick. I had bronchitis once so bad I almost lost my voice, but I could not go to a doctor. I had no one to stay with him. He soon forgot my name. He got out of the house a few times, and I would have a hard time getting him back home. He would get angry. He always thought he was going home. He needed someone to take him out riding or something. I couldn't do that by myself.

I was so exhausted taking care of him. You don't get to sleep day or night, just nap when you can. They call it a thirty-six-hour day. I say the day never ends.

He had to take so much medicine for his lungs and heart. I believe that was some of his trouble. He was in the hospital an awful lot.

One of my daughters, Debra, would take off from work a night occasionally and spend the night so I could rest. His son stayed a few nights and his grandson Carey helped me all he could. He happened to be there one night when JW pulled a heavy picture off the wall. When I screamed, Carey jumped out of bed and ran across the hall to him and caught the picture before it hurt either one of us. I couldn't believe he got there so quickly.

One night, JW got up in a chair and got his pistol from a shelf in his bedroom closet. He remembered where he kept it. He had forgotten how to unload it, but he banged it on the bedpost and floor until it came open. I was standing right beside him, and when it opened, there was a shell in every hole. Why it didn't go off or why he never pulled the trigger is still a mystery to me.

Then he shook the shells out and went into another room for something. It gave me time to pick the shells up and put them in my pocket. I got his new box and hid them also. When he came back, he hunted for the shells and got back in the chair, hunting for the new box. He remembered having them.

The next morning, I gave them to his son. I did not want them in the house. He was real good with guns.

He told me one of us was sick, but I couldn't figure out which one it was. The only time his memory came back he was sitting in the swing out in the yard with someone, and he came in the house. I was fixing something to eat. He came up to me and put his arms around me and told me to come and sit on the couch with him a while so he could love me while he could. Those times are hard to forget, so very few. He didn't sit there very long until the stranger was there again, and he never left again.

One Sunday night, rain was pouring down. He wanted to go to church. I didn't want to get out in the rain, but he was determined to go. He kept on until he found the car keys, and the door key was with them. He was going by himself.

I knew he couldn't drive, and I couldn't get him back in the house, so I started with him. It was already late, but when we got close to the church, the police had closed the road to the church off. We couldn't get through. I turned around and started back home, and he was trying to get me to go another way. I didn't know my way around Nashville, especially at night and driving in the rain. He got so angry. When we got home, he was going to walk. He went out on the porch. I just told him to go on. In a few minutes, he came back inside and went to bed for a little while.

The next morning, his son came by. I told him the way JW wanted to go. He said I couldn't have gone that way. It would have taken me uptown. He was glad I came back home.

During this time, I had this dream. I dreamed I went into a strange room. All my children were standing together in the middle of it. Fred, my first husband, was in there also.

I looked at Judy. I felt like he had come after her. She said, "No, Mama, he came after you."

I went over to him. We went up in a tunnel. A pretty black-haired lady was with us. I looked at the children standing there, and she said to me, "It is hard to leave them."

I said, "Yes, it is."

Then she said, "I'll go with you." I truly believe that was our baby girl we lost so many years ago. She had black hair also.

When we got up there, we went through a cloud to a half circle of the most beautiful green grass I had ever seen. So many people were sitting in it, laughing and talking—men and women. She and Fred went in and sat down with them. I was standing in a path around it with a few others. Behind them I could see through the cloud what looked like an enormous building full of windows.

Then I heard a man's voice say, "She can go back now."

Fred stood up and said, "I'll show her the way." Then he came over to me and said, "Now you can go back," and in a flash, we were back in the room. The children were standing just like we left them. Then just like the wind picked him up, Fred was gone, and I woke up.

I thought about that dream. It was so plain, and I thought I saw Bertha Dee and Fred, but I didn't see Fred Allen the little seventeen-and-one-half-month-old son we lost.

Then in a week or so, I dreamed again. I was in a big field, and there was only one house, no other in sight—a big farmhouse with a porch all across the front of it. I was sitting on the edge of the porch with my feet on the ground. I have never seen a van like the one that was parked in front of the house. It was so large.

Two young men brought a beautiful couch out of the house and took it around to the other side of the van to load it. Then a young woman came around the van to the side next to me and opened the doors on that side. It had a lot of shelves and all of them were filled with covered dishes and containers of prepared food ready to eat.

I said to her, "You don't have to stop at restaurants when you travel to eat."

She said, "No, we eat when we want to."

Then she came over to where I was sitting on the porch and said to me, "That young man who is helping load our things is an angel, and when our things are loaded, he is going back to heaven."

I asked her if she would ask him to come over and talk to me before he left. She said yes, she would, and she did.

In a few seconds, here he came. He came up to me. He leaned over me and smiled. He never said one word. I reached up and pulled his head down and kissed him on his forehead. Then I said to him, "Now I can say I have kissed an angel." Then like the wind, he floated back and was gone, and I woke up. I believe it was Fred Allen.

I don't understand those dreams. I was in so much stress. I believe the Lord gave me those dreams to comfort me, and I praise Him for them. They gave me strength and hope during that tragic time—a glimpse of heaven and my loved ones there.

Not long after that, I saw JW going down the street as fast as he could walk. I ran a long way to catch up with him. He told me he was going home. I begged him to come back with me, but he wouldn't. If I caught a hold of his hand, he would jerk away. I kept on until he got angry, then he turned around and walked back so fast I couldn't keep up with him. When he got nearly to the house, he stopped. He said to me, "I've been thinking. You go your way, and I'll go my way." I told him "Okay, but let's go and sit in the swing and talk about it." So he went with me. He thought I was trying to boss him around because I didn't want him to get out and get lost or hurt. I was the big bad one. I was completely exhausted.

While we were sitting there, Gwen and Tuck came by. They were going to the mountains to see Judy and Freddy. They wanted us to go with them, and he wanted to go, so we went with them. We stayed two or three days. He enjoyed himself. He ate well while we were there.

He did little things to hurt me and said some pretty bad things to them about me. He wouldn't let me touch him. The only time was when he needed me. I was the one who took care of him (the big bad wolf). I did everything I could for him. I knew it wasn't him acting like that. He was a kind, loving man, and that was what hurt me so bad. He didn't even know who I was, not even my name. Some days he was pretty alert, but that wasn't very often.

The Sunday afternoon when we came home, he sat out on the porch a long time and talked to one of our neighbors. I went on in the house and sat down on the couch. When he came in the house, he passed by me. Instead of sitting down with me, he started across the room to the chair he nearly always sat in.

I really don't know what happened. It was so fast. As he went to sit down, he just whirled across the floor to the other side of the room. He fell into my quilt I was quilting (I was quilting these little over the lap frames) and then into the TV. The quilt helped break his fall.

I ran to him and helped him up, and I said, "I'm so glad it didn't hurt you," but he said it did. Then I noticed his forehead was bleeding so badly. I had a hard time stopping the blood. He also broke his arm.

I couldn't get hold of anyone to take him to a doctor. His son came up the next morning and took him. They put a cast on, but later I made them take it off. It got bad sore under it, and he was suffering so badly. In a few days, he was in the hospital again. He got pneumonia, and his lungs were so bad. He didn't live very much longer. He would tell me how bad he felt, but he wouldn't tell his son. Sometimes I think Wayne thought it was me who was so bad. But I finally got him to tell Wayne.

When he left the hospital, the doctor wouldn't let him come home. He said, "I had taken enough. I couldn't stand anymore." He told Wayne he could take him to his house, but they took him to a nursing home close to his son. It wasn't close to me, and I couldn't see him. My daughter Debbie and his daughter-in-law said he knew everything the day he died and asked who was with me.

June 22 was his birthday, and Debbie took off from work and surprised him at the hospital with a birthday party. She brought a cake, drinks, candles, and ice cream—everything—and the nurses on his floor came in and sang happy birthday for him and some ate cake with him. He was so happy.

My little granddaughter Valerie was leaving for church camp. She went to the window, looked out, and started singing "Amazing Grace," and he started singing it with her. He sang it every day after that until he died. He passed away on July 3.

Debbie went to see him that night and brought him a milkshake and held it while he drank it. He was dead the next morning when they went in to check on him.

He only lived four days after they took him to the nursing home. He was buried in the Harpeth Hills Cemetery beside Wayne's mother, Mildred.

He was a precious little man. I really miss him.

After JW passed away, it was too lonely for me there in that big house alone. I stayed about one year in and out of the house. I was so lonely, and I didn't feel safe there anymore. I was right beside a park. Sometimes mischief-makers would cause trouble, but they never bothered me.

I pretended I was all right, but every night I would put a Bible in front of every door and pray over it for God to protect me, then I would go to bed and go to sleep. It wasn't good for me to be there alone. I was too nervous.

One morning, about eight o'clock, I was sitting in the middle of my bed looking at my flowers. I had put them in the corner of my bedroom so they could get the morning sun. They were so beautiful. I was worrying. I knew if I moved, I couldn't take them or all of them. While I was sitting there looking at them, a man came walking across my room. He walked right into my flowers and disappeared, vanished. He had his hands up over the side of his face. But I could tell you the color of his clothes. He was fully dressed.

The funniest thing is it didn't even frighten me. I was praying for God to protect me, and I truly believe He did. I love the Lord and thank Him.

I moved to Dandridge Towers on June 8, 1995, another lonely place.

GOD GAVE ME AN ANGEL

by Lisa Teller

God gave me an angel right here on earth,
She taught me my values and gave me self-worth,
She guides me through life with her wisdom, God's light,
She steers me from wrong, and leads me toward right.

She stands by my side when things are rough,
She taught me in bad times we need to be tough.
She is there when I need her throughout all my years,
She laughed with me in happy times, and comforted my tears.

My angel on earth was sent from above,
God paid her not in wages, but with eternal love.
She has been my confidante, my rock, my protector,
And when God says her job is through, I know I won't forget her.

She need not a halo, or silken wings of grace,
For the glory of God's love shines upon her face.
My Guardian angel, can be replaced by no other,
She is God's gift to me—I call her my dear mother.

About the Author

Minnie Belle Webb was born on March 3, 1916, in Cullman, Alabama. However, she lived most of her life in Middle Tennessee. She would tell the story of how she and her sister got caught in a cattle drive down Main Street in Columbia, Tennessee, and had to climb the nearest tree to watch the spectacle pass.

Motherhood was her greatest calling. While still very young, she met Fred Webb. It was love at first sight. They married and had ten children.

Her family was always her highest priority. She spent most of her life raising and caring for her children and grandchildren that followed. She was always available when anyone needed a shoulder and some godly advice. Her greatest desire was to bring glory to God in her daily life and to raise her children to love and to serve Him.

She began to write her book of memories while in her eighties and finished just before her death at ninety. Her utmost wish would be for her stories to minister to everyone who reads them.